The short guide to community development

D1459266

Alison Gilchrist and Marilyn Taylor

First published in Great Britain in 2011 by

The Policy Press
University of Bristol
Fourth Floor
Beacon House
Queen's Road
Bristol BS8 1QU
UK

t: +44 (0)117 331 4054
f: +44 (0)117 331 4093
tpp-info@bristol.ac.uk
www.policypress.co.uk

North American office:
The Policy Press
c/o International Specialized Books Services
920 NE 58th Avenue, Suite 300
Portland, OR 97213-3786, USA
t: +1 503 287 3093
f: +1 503 280 8832
info@isbs.com

303812

Contents

List of tables and boxes

Tables

Boxes

1

introduction

'Community' is a concept that seems always to be in fashion with policy makers – community development less so. In some quarters, the existence of community is seen as a natural and enduring facet of society; others lament its decline. One of the primary purposes of community development is to boost the effectiveness of community participation and capacity. Not everyone sees the necessity of strategic interventions to achieve this. Indeed, the term itself is problematic, with the approach also being called social development, popular education, critical pedagogy, community organising, community engagement and community education. In the UK, some writers prefer the term 'critical community practice' (Butcher et al, 2007), which describes a broader approach to working with communities. Nonetheless, internationally, community development is commonly adopted by non-governmental organisations as a means of developing infrastructure, local economic initiatives and democracy. Governments worldwide, too, have introduced community development programmes to tackle poverty and other seemingly intractable social problems. They have also been confronted by communities which have decided to mobilise for themselves, organising services, protest actions and self-help movements to improve living standards and gain important civil rights.

In the 1950s, the United Nations defined community development as 'a process designed to create conditions of economic and social progress for the whole community with its active participation' (United Nations, 1955). More recently, successive conferences organised by the International Association for Community Development have issued statements describing community development as:

> a way of strengthening civil society by prioritising the actions of
> communities and their perspectives in the development of social, economic
> and environmental policy ... It strengthens the capacity of people as active
> citizens through their own groups, organisations and networks ... to work
> in dialogue [and] plays a crucial role in supporting active democratic life
> by promoting the autonomous voice of disadvantaged and vulnerable
> communities (Craig et al, 2004; Craig and Mak, 2007; Dorsner, 2008).

Within the UK, the fortunes and status of community development
have waxed and waned. As an external intervention, it was initially used
by philanthropic bodies (for example, the university Settlements) to
bring adult education and capacity building to deprived neighbourhoods,
such as the London docklands. Local authorities and housing trusts
later employed officers in new towns and estates to encourage
residents to set up groups and associations for various leisure and civic
purposes as a way of engendering 'community spirit' and promoting
self-help. For a long time, it raised for policy makers the spectre of
the Community Development Projects in the 1970s (Loney, 1983),
a government-sponsored programme whose Marxist critique of
capitalism – despite striking a chord with many practitioners – was
not quite what the programme's sponsors had in mind. More recently,
community development has been used to build 'community capacity'
and 'social capital', as well as to support 'community empowerment' and
participation as part of new approaches to persistent local problems.
As we write, the UK government is embracing another term in the
community portfolio – community organising, an approach that came
to prominence as part of Barack Obama's successful bid for the US
presidency.

Community development is not a term that necessarily travels well.
In the global South it retains its colonial connotations, devoid of the
political content that characterises popular education movements,
say, in Latin America (Pearce et al, 2010). In India, a special issue of
Community Development Journal is called 'Community Organisation
in India' (vol 44 no 3). Elsewhere, however, the term maintains its
currency. In the US, where 'community development corporations
are increasingly assuming the roles of local government' (De Filippis

and Saegert, 2007), it describes a mainstream set of practices and institutions. It also continues to have salience in a number of OECD countries, such as Australia and Canada.

There are of course many debates about the terminology of community and community development and we will visit these in the chapters that follow. In an earlier introduction to community development, in which one of us was involved, we argued that community development:

> seeks to release the potential within communities. It does this by bringing people together to address issues of common concern and to develop the skills, confidence and resources to address these problems. In doing so, it can strengthen relationships within the community and encourage people to use their energies and resources more effectively at local level. This is now often referred to as 'capacity building'. Second it works ... to change the relationships between people in communities and the institutions that shape their lives'. (Taylor et al 2000, p 3)

But this underplays the strong emphasis on values in many definitions. A quick review of definitions that have been developed by scholars, practitioners and institutions concerned with community development yields a number of common themes concerned with social change, social justice, collective action, equality and mutual respect, enabling, and changing power relationships. A recent US reader echoes the analysis of the Community Development Projects in the UK, arguing that: 'Community development occurs when the conditions of surviving and thriving in a place are not being supplied by capital'. It highlights the need to connect geographical communities to the 'far greater resources, opportunities and power that lie outside [them]' (De Filippis and Saegert, 2007). Definitions from elsewhere in the world emphasise the need to develop political awareness alongside skills, confidence and resources, drawing on the popular education movement in Latin America and the seminal writings of Paulo Freire.

As the statement below shows, many definitions acknowledge the need to work with the assets and experience that communities already have rather than working with the deficit model that policy makers tend to assume.

| **Box 1.1** | **What is community development?** |

Community development can be both an occupation (such as a community development worker in a local authority) and a way of working with communities. Its key purpose is to build communities based on *justice, equality* and *mutual respect*.

Community development involves changing the relationships between ordinary people and people in positions of power, so that everyone can take part in the issues that affect their lives. It starts from the principle that within any community there is a wealth of knowledge and experience which, if used in creative ways, can be channelled into collective action to achieve the communities' desired goals.

Community development practitioners work alongside people in communities to help build relationships with key people and organisations and to identify common concerns. They create opportunities for the community to learn new skills and, by enabling people to act together, community development practitioners help to foster social inclusion and equality.

Source: www.cdx.org.uk/community-development/what-community-development (emphases in original)

There is some debate over whether community development is an approach, an occupation or a movement. Is it a profession of specialist workers or does it simply indicate a particular way of working in or with communities? Is it about the creation of resources, capacity, infrastructure and leadership for communities to use in whichever ways they choose? Or is it a set of techniques that can be used to accomplish externally defined objectives? Is it a movement for social change? Or is it about the development of 'community' itself? By this, we mean fostering the sense of belonging and collective efficacy that people sometimes express as providing security, practical help and emotional support from those around them – friends, neighbours but also more casual acquaintances drawn from everyday interactions and activities. For many, community supplies both the focus and motivation for people to organise to get things done and to press for change. The function that community plays in people's lives and in policy will be a theme that we return to throughout the book, examining how community development skills and support are understood and applied by activists, professionals, policy makers and philanthropists to tackle the social, economic and political challenges that face so many post-industrial societies.

In this Short Guide, we start in Chapter Two by reviewing definitions and understandings of community development, describing different models and how they differ from related approaches and concepts. The next two chapters look at context and theory. Chapter Three lays out the policies and other factors that have shaped community development over the years and the policy themes that it is expected to address. In Chapter Four, we review some of the theories that can help inform community development practice, focusing particularly on theories of community, the state, collective organising and power. Chapters Five and Six come back to the practice of community development. Chapter Five considers the skills, values and techniques that constitute community development practice, how to do it and the infrastructure that is needed to support it; Chapter Six describes how it can be applied in different policy fields. The final two chapters explore the challenges that face community development. Chapter Seven looks at the issues and dilemmas that are inherent within its practice and strategic approach, while Chapter Eight looks at the way external trends are likely to affect its development.

The Guide is written from a British perspective. We have referred to experience and debates elsewhere in the world, particularly in the US, and we believe that many of the issues raised have a wider significance.

But community development is to some extent dependent on context, and though its potential is worldwide, strategies will vary between regions. However, we end by welcoming the increasing willingness of community development workers in the global North – and policy makers too – to learn from practice in the global South.

This last comment raises some more language issues. Most of the terminology that distinguishes between different regions of the world is problematic: thankfully the 'third world' has all but disappeared from our vocabulary, but how do we describe the distinction that used to be made between the developed and developing worlds? With apologies to Australasia, we have chosen to use the terms global South and global North.

Finally, while we are on the subject of terminology, we need to say how we are using the term 'community'. We know that communities are multi-faceted and may be fragmented, so to talk of 'community' or even 'communities' implies a homogeneity that cannot be assumed. However, in the absence of a clearer term, we have decided to refer to the people that community development works with as communities or community members.

Our intention with this Short Guide is to demonstrate both the versatility and value of community development to modern society, but also to examine the many ways in which it is contested and challenged by political critiques and practical circumstances. Our broad conclusion is that community development has a great deal to offer communities and professionals working across a whole range of policy goals. For it to be effective and sustainable, however, it needs a strategic investment in the skills, resources and infrastructure that are essential if communities are to play their part in building a more equitable and democratic society.

Further reading

There have been few comprehensive guides to community development published in book form in recent years. At the time of writing, Alan Twelvetrees' updated edition of *Community work* (2008) is probably the most recent, and the reader will find a strong account of a Freire-based approach to community development in Margaret Ledwith's 2005 book, *Community development*. Perhaps the most comprehensive is Keith Popple's book (1995), though this is now some 15 years old. Readers will also find much of interest in *Critical community practice*, by Butcher et al (2007).

To gain a comprehensive overview of the evolution of community development over time, both in practice and in theory, readers are advised to go to three excellent readers published over the last few years. An international perspective is provided by Gary Craig, Keith Popple and Mae Shaw in *Community development in theory and practice* (2008), which brings together a collection of articles from the international *Community Development Journal*, since its inception in 1965. A US perspective is provided by James De Filippis and Susan Saegert in their *Community development reader* (2007). Gary Craig and co-editors have also published a UK reader, *The community development reader: History, themes and issues* (2011), drawing together influential articles and book extracts from a variety of sources from the 1950s to the present day.

Finally, two journals also provide a valuable source: *Community Development Journal* and *Community Development*, the journal of the US-based Community Development Society. Readers will also find valuable material in development studies journals, *Development Studies* itself and the *IDS Bulletin*, published by the Institute of Development Studies. *Concept: The Journal of Contemporary Community Education Practice Theory* is another useful source. It is now published online, but a collection of key articles from its first 16 years have been published by Mae Shaw, Jane Meagher and Stuart Moir in *Participation in community development: Problems and possibilities* (2006).

2

what is community development?

This chapter focuses on definitions and different understandings of community development, in particular distinguishing community development from related approaches and concepts. It sets out the core principles and processes associated with community development and reviews different classifications and models for working with communities to achieve change as well as exploring the relationship between community development and related approaches.

Underpinning principles and processes

As we saw in Chapter One, community development represents a broad approach to working with people in communities to achieve greater levels of social justice. In the main, the focus is on individuals, groups and networks that want or need to cooperate in order to achieve change at a local or community level. That change might be driven by an external threat to people's quality of life (for example, the building of new housing on a much-loved green space) or it could be shaped by residents' desire to improve services for a particular section of the community (for example providing something for young people to distract them from drugs or vandalism). Adopting a community development approach means ensuring that the issues and priorities are identified and agreed by the communities themselves, and that people are encouraged to work together towards a collective solution to a shared concern. There are three vital aspects of community development:

■ informal education
■ collective action
■ organisation development.

Informal education describes the learning that takes place predominantly through direct involvement in community activities, and so it is sometimes described as experiential. People learn new skills through taking on tasks, observing others, 'having a go' and receiving feedback. They acquire useful knowledge by listening to discussion, maybe having something explained that they need to know, or by finding out from reports and pamphlets. Having assumptions challenged through questioning and debate can result in people gaining new understanding and insights that contradict what they have learnt at school or from friends. Learning and practice increases people's confidence, their openness to new ideas and their ability to take on unfamiliar roles and responsibilities. For many people, participation in community development activities represents an important step on the journey to active citizenship or a career goal. It is also about learning to question received wisdom and to challenge authority.

Box. 2.1   Jatinder's journey

Jatinder joins a playgroup being run at her older child's school so that the toddler can learn to socialise. After a few months of regular attendance, she joins the committee and at the annual meeting is persuaded to take on the role of treasurer. She is initially reluctant as she was not good with figures at school, but the community worker persuades her by talking through the role and explaining how to set up a simple accounting system to keep track of the money coming in (mainly from membership fees and the occasional small grant) and the spending. Despite her earlier difficulties, Jatinder finds that she is able to do this task easily and that she actually enjoys working with numbers. She is helped by the community worker to prepare the accounts for the committee. She agrees to represent the group on the local under-fives forum and is invited to go on a course to learn computer-based book-keeping. She enjoys this so much that she takes responsibility for running the family business accounts and later gets a job as ledger clerk for a small firm. They are so impressed by her enthusiasm and ability that after a couple of years they agree to pay her fees and give her study leave to undertake her accountancy qualifications. Now that her children are at school, she has taken the plunge and runs her own successful accounting business, specialising in support for community groups.

A central theme of community development is that it supports people to take collective action to tackle problems that many individuals may be experiencing or to help achieve a shared dream that many will benefit from. This does not necessarily require setting up a formal organisation. It could involve bringing several groups together as a campaigning alliance or in some kind of coalition arrangement around a shared goal. The important point is that people are not left to fend for themselves, to make complaints or put forward suggestions as isolated residents. Community development works with people to identify the aims they have in common and supports them to accomplish these. Community development often provides the impetus to mobilise community members to develop a joint plan of action, recruit allies and activists and decide what needs to be done to make the changes they want. It is about finding the power of combined voices and determination; the strength of many people acting for their mutual benefit or to champion the interests of those who cannot stand up for themselves.

Just as individuals develop their capacity, so organisations sometimes need to develop to meet the changing demands of members and the expectations of other stakeholders, such as funders. In community development, developing an organisation means helping it to evolve a form that enables the members to achieve their goals, to act legally and to be accountable to the membership and wider community. This may occur in response to a crisis when people realise that the existing format simply doesn't work any more or it may unfold more organically.

Community development helps with these kinds of transitions, enabling discussion with members about what's going wrong or what could be done differently.

A familiar situation arises when a community group has achieved or outgrown its original objectives and wants to take on more ambitious aims. It has a number of options at this juncture: staying the same with limited aspirations, setting up a new group to pursue the new goals, changing the nature of the group to become more formal and public, or possibly linking up with other similar organisations. Difficulties often occur because members do not always recognise the need for change or they disagree about the next phase of development. So, for example, a worker might assist a relatively informal group or network to discuss their next steps, to consider alternatives and perhaps agree to become a properly constituted organisation. If the community members decide that they want to set up a formal body, the worker can help them choose a suitable structure, to establish a clear and common purpose and to decide how any office bearers (chair, secretary, etc) are going to be democratically elected and held to account. This may involve setting up the organisation as a legal entity, such as a community interest company, a limited company or a friendly society in order to safeguard both money and members. Sometimes, an organisation needs to grow new structures as the range of its activities expands. For example, a community association might decide to set up a subcommittee to deal with the work it does with young people, or to run an annual event such as a street party. As it matures and takes on paid employees, it may find it needs a separate group to oversee the recruitment and management of staff.

Providing help, building on resources

Each of the three aspects listed in the previous section is about building the skills, knowledge and confidence of individuals as well as developing the infrastructure to support community organising and engagement. Community development is sometimes criticised as working from a deficit model, which assumes that communities lack capacity or leadership, and that these need to be either imported from experts or nurtured through support and training. To a certain extent, this has some resonance with the approach of many professionals and yet it undervalues the wealth of energy, skills and local knowledge that community members pour into their activities and campaigns. The assets-based model of community development, which is examined later in this chapter (Kretzmann and McKnight, 1993), offers a more positive counter approach. However, there are still specific areas of expertise and technical advice that community development workers are able to provide or refer people to, for example on charity law, planning regulations or fundraising. They often have time to do things that community members are too busy for, or can provide a useful external perspective on disputes or difficulties. Their accumulated experience and training in how groups work, the various functions of organisations and the complex dynamics of communities can act as a resource which is 'on tap' but not 'on top'.

In other words, community workers are there to serve the interests of communities, and to help them gain greater influence over decisions that affect their lives. In the early years of community development, there was a vigorous debate over how 'directive' the workers should be, with some arguing that they should be completely neutral, responding entirely to the communities' expressed needs and aspirations, in the ultimate empowering role (see Batten and Batten, 1967). More recently, as we will see below and in Chapter Seven, there has been acknowledgement that the workers usually do have an agenda, driven to some extent by their employer's policies and priorities, but also by occupational values and principles (FCDL, 2009a). Their work will inevitably be influenced by their own interests, capabilities, preferences and 'theories of change'.

Community development's core values

Community development is often described as a long-term value-based process. Its overarching purpose is to promote social justice and it is therefore steeped in politics (with a small 'p'). However, social justice is a tricky term to define, tending to mean whatever its proponents want it to mean. Within community development, it is usually understood as the development of a more equal society, with wealth, opportunities and power more evenly distributed across the population.

In practice this means that community development demonstrates an awareness of the structural inequalities that currently shape society. These are generally associated with class, gender, 'race', disability, sexual orientation and age, referring to the most prevalent patterns of discrimination and those covered by the UK's equalities legislation. Equality is therefore seen as a core value for community development, and practitioners are expected to incorporate anti-discriminatory measures into all aspects of their work (Gilchrist, 2007; FCDL, 2009a). This means adapting arrangements and practice to take into account the diversity of participants or target communities. Because community development is often seen as remedial, focused on supposed problems and deficits, projects and workers tend to be located in areas where the whole community is stigmatised and excluded. These might be where there has been social breakdown or enduring failures of the local economy, often in inner cities or peripheral estates, though rural deprivation is also a major issue. Within these populations, there will be further inequalities and tensions caused by different forms of oppression, such as xenophobia or ageism.

Community development places great emphasis on participation and empowerment: community members being involved directly in decision making about what happens in their areas of interest and people's capacity to influence those decisions being increased through active steps to open up democratic processes to wider involvement. This applies as much at community level as in the arenas of civil society and local and national government. Thus community development workers will try to ensure that those who tend to be excluded or marginalised from decisions are encouraged to put forward their views and to have these respected. For example, children and young people find formal meetings alien, so other ways might be found to elicit their ideas and worries, such as using drawing or 'speakout' sessions. Levels of empowerment can be usefully envisaged as a ladder or pyramid, with increasing influence for communities depending in part on the actions and attitudes of the 'power holders' and in part on the confidence and capacity of the community members involved. As we shall see in Chapter Four, this can range from tokenistic attempts to engage people in 'invited spaces' where the 'rules of the game' and sometimes even the outcomes are already determined, to genuine control of resources and decisions. Community development should aim for communities to be as far towards the 'empowered' or 'in control' end of the spectrum as is feasible in the given circumstances.

As indicated earlier, collective working and cooperation are also key principles of community development, so wherever possible community workers encourage individuals, groups and organisations to work together, informally or through partnership arrangements, to achieve aims that they have in common. They may well play a brokering role in making the links between different agencies or parts of the community, identifying potential synergies and mediating latent rivalries or tensions.

As a result of community development's commitment to learning and capacity building, it recognises the value of reflection and dialogue. Throughout our lives, we learn in many different ways: teaching, studying, trial and error, experimentation, observation, practice and deliberation. Most of us need feedback and encouragement from others, especially our peers. Community development workers, like youth and play workers, actively support and contribute to informal education by getting people to think about their experiences, try out new skills, question assumptions and explore new ways of seeing the world. Only by understanding how things are now is it possible to change them for the better.

An integrated approach

One model offered for looking at these various principles is to think of community development as way of working *with* communities, which combines six integrated roles (see Table 2.1).

In essence, this model is about enhancing the relationship between the people and the state. It assumes that for communities to gain more influence over decision making and to become more able to design and deliver their own services, they may need external support and advice, as well as securing improvements in how the state is able to listen to and learn from community perspectives.

Related models

The approach described earlier is most commonly practised in the UK, but there are other models which have gained ascendancy and are popular here and in other parts of the world. Some are more radical than others and are based on different theories of change. Several authors have developed useful typologies or frameworks to describe these (Rothman and Tropman, 1968; Popple, 1995; Smock, 2003). Broadly speaking, the categories reflect different analyses of society and different overall goals. (See Chapter Four for more detailed explanations of the theory behind these political models.) The three approaches described below can be seen as:

(A) fundamentally changing the way society operates;
(B) rebalancing the system to be fairer and more democratic; and
(C) making the existing structures work more smoothly.

(A) Fundamentally changing the way society operates

Radical models are concerned with the root causes of injustice and inequality. These approaches are informed by an explanation of power that places it in the hands of elites or vested interests. On the

Table 2.1: Six components for community development

Role	Outcome
1. Help people see that they have common concerns about local or other public issues that they could benefit from working on together under their own control	Reduction of isolation and alienation Increase in social capital[1] and cooperation
2. Help people to work together on those issues, often by forming or developing an independent community group, supporting them to plan and take actions and encouraging evaluation and reflection as a way of improving effectiveness	Creation or improvement of bona fide community groups Increase of opportunities for activity in the community More effective community activity Strengthened community sector Increased volunteering Mutual aid and autonomous services
3. Support and develop networking between communities and independent groups across the community sector and build links with voluntary sector bodies	Learning between groups More effective voice for communities Increased 'bridging' social capital and community cohesion Improvement in conditions in the locality

[1] Social capital has been defined by the UK Office for National Statistics as 'the pattern and intensity of networks among people and the shared values which arise from those networks'. It is discussed in more detail in Chapter Four.

Table 2.1: continued

Role	Outcome
4. Promote values of equity, inclusiveness, participation and cooperation throughout this work	Increase in: Participation Social capital Collaboration More equal relations and outcomes for disadvantaged communities
5. Empower people and their organisations to influence and transform public policies and services and all factors affecting the conditions of their lives	Community engagement and influence Improvement in dialogue between community and authorities Improvement in coherence and effectiveness of public policies
6. Advise and inform public authorities on community perspectives and assist them to strengthen communities and work in genuine partnership with them	Increased capacity of agencies, authorities and professions to engage with communities Improvement in delivery of public services Increased resources for the community sector

Source: Adapted from *Community development challenge* (CLG, 2006, p 17)

one hand, the Alinsky model of community organising tends to be oppositional, mobilising communities to confront the 'power holders' in an attempt to negotiate change from a position of collective strength and solidarity (Alinksy, 1972). Alinsky and his disciples operated by building relationships at the grassroots, recruiting and training indigenous leaders to act as organisers, and uniting different parts of the communities in a broad alliance around a common cause. The starting point is always the practical concerns and grievances expressed by communities themselves, but the goal may be to redistribute power in favour of disadvantaged people in low income communities, using a pragmatic assessment of ends and means. A frequently adopted tactic is to express mass dissent through protest, often focused on a single person (such as the boss of a major polluting industry) or through imaginative direct actions which expose injustices and demand change.

> As an organizer I start from where the world is, as it is, not as I would like it to be. That we accept the world as it is does not in any sense weaken our desire to change it into what we believe it should be – it is necessary to begin where the world is if we are going to change it to what we think it should be. That means working in the system. (Alinsky, 1972, p xix).

Citizen organising has been highly successful in some of England's bigger cities and has found favour with the current government, which sees it as a means to create the 'Big Society' in which services are run by communities through voluntary effort and social enterprise (see Chapter Three).

An alternative model, usually associated with Freire (1972), aims to transform the political basis of society through education and reflective action. This approach, based on critical dialogue, has been used to support informal, popular or community education among communities which are poor or oppressed. By taking part in facilitated, ongoing conversations, people learn to question what they have been told and become aware of injustices in their lives (termed conscientisation), as well as possibilities for radical change driven by community action. This model has become known as social pedagogy and is associated with a commitment to praxis, that is, action based on informed and considered thinking. It is transformational in that it aims to create systemic change, challenging the prevailing ideologies and leading to an alternative vision for society (Smock, 2003; Ledwith and Springett, 2010).

(B) Rebalancing the system to be fairer and more democratic

Community development strategies are more often based on liberal pluralist models, which acknowledge that society is made up of an array of interest groups who organise collectively to compete for attention, influence and resources. Pluralism is explored more fully in Chapter Four. Model B is concerned with making sure that a full range of experience and perspectives is included in decisions about how resources are allocated or services designed. It recognises that not all groups have equal access to power and that certain disadvantaged sections of society need additional support and resources in order for their voices and their views to influence decision makers. In this respect, a key role for community development is to address structural inequalities and attempt to create a more level playing field for members of the community who are oppressed or marginalised. The state is seen as a neutral body, overseeing these negotiations between different interests, with decisions made in accordance with a rational appraisal of the evidence, based on the arguments put forward by diverse stakeholders. The pluralist model of community development aims for reforms that lead to a fairer distribution of power in society generally, as well as at the grassroots.

In some respects, user empowerment falls into this model, whereby service commissioners and providers make available support and mechanisms to enable users to influence delivery and priorities in spending. For example, a social landlord, such as a housing association, might find it expedient to encourage tenants to contribute to decision making about how its properties are managed so that ideas for improvement are captured and there is a greater sense of collective responsibility for the upkeep of the estate, including standards of neighbourly behaviour. There is no question of challenging the ownership and control of the landlord, simply of helping things to run more smoothly in the interests of both parties. Community engagement represents a parallel model that is open to wider participation and generally not focused on specific services. It is a stronger version of consultation, by which public authorities seek to involve citizens in planning improvements and addressing longstanding problems. Community engagement requires changes in the culture and procedures of institutions such as local councils or health foundations to render them more 'community friendly' and accessible. Effective and inclusive engagement practices *should* result in community empowerment – community development values and expertise can make a real difference to the successful implementation of user empowerment and community engagement.

Both these approaches favour negotiation and compromise rather than conflict. The role of the community development worker, sometimes called participation or engagement officer, is to support community members or service users to develop a collective voice and present a persuasive case. To this end community-led action research can provide evidence to sway the argument. Communities are involved in every aspect of the research process, from deciding the aims, through collecting data, to analysing and presenting the findings. The intention is to demonstrate the impact of particular actions (interventions) and thereby to identify innovative solutions to shared problems. A related approach is known as participatory appraisal. It has been extensively used in the rural areas of developing countries (Chambers, 1994) and is beginning to be adopted by some authorities in the UK. Essentially, participatory appraisal uses a set of creative, flexible techniques designed to involve as many people as possible in mapping an area's problems, setting priorities and devising solutions. An advantage lies in training community members in these methods so that they can select those most appropriate to the situation and facilitate the process themselves. The role of the agency is to listen, learn and respond to community experiences rather than coming in with preconceived interventions. This allows a greater sense of ownership of proposed strategies and increases the likelihood that they will work in the given circumstances and be sustained by the people themselves.

(C) Making the existing structures work more smoothly

The third family of community development methods relies on a conservative or functionalist model of society and is more likely to maintain the overall status quo. There is a communitarian emphasis on enabling people to exercise mutual rights and responsibilities, without challenging the general order of things. This approach, which is reflected in some aspects of the Big Society thinking, aims to strengthen community spirit and build the capacity of local groups and networks to contribute independently to civil society or to work in partnership with state or voluntary agencies. It highlights the positive features of communities rather than their failings, but draws attention to what might happen if shared responsibilities are neglected. Communitarian approaches are designed to mobilise the resources, enthusiasm and efforts of 'ordinary' residents, with one well-known model describing itself as asset-based community development (ABCD) because it focuses on the strengths rather than the weaknesses of communities (Kretzmann and McKnight, 1993). This comprehensive approach to community building is based on the belief that the role of community development is to assist communities to become self-reliant and cohesive, participating in civil society as a unified body of active citizens. Its starting point is to undertake an inventory of individual or household skills, interests and experience to gauge the combined potential capacity of the community.

This model should not be confused with the 'Achieving better community development' approach to planning and evaluation, which shares the same acronym (Barr and Hashagen, 2000); see Chapter Seven.

Every single person has capabilities, abilities and gifts. Living a good life depends on whether those capabilities can be used, abilities expressed and gifts given. If they are, such people will be valued, feel powerful and be well-connected to the people around them. And the community around the person will be more powerful because of the contribution that person is making.

Each time a person uses his or her capacity, the community is stronger and the person more powerful. That is why strong communities are basically places where the capacities of local residents are identified, valued and used. Weak communities are places that fail, for whatever reason, to mobilize the skills, capacities and talents of their residents or members. (Kretzmann and McKnight, 2003, p 1)

The ABCD model (as it has become known) is interested in assets rather than needs, but as a consequence, it fails to address the political dimensions that cause needs and problems in the first place. In this it bears a strong resemblance to the civic model proposed by Smock (2003), which she identifies as promoting informal mechanisms for maintaining social order within deprived or diverse neighbourhoods, pre-empting disturbances and attempting to 'bridge' divisions between different sections of the community in the name of stability and consensus. The processes for achieving this could include the establishment of community forums, alongside the development of mediation and conflict resolution skills among key local residents.

All of these approaches to working with communities use elements of community development that can be applied with a light touch (Taylor et al, 2007) or within a more general programme of interventions. Thus different professional services, such as health promotion, housing management, youth work, neighbourhood policing, social care, regeneration and so on use community development methods and might be informed to some extent by its values. Chapter Six gives examples of how community development can be applied in a range of policy areas and settings.

The term community practice was introduced by Butcher et al (1993) to distinguish this form of working from community development, with its emphasis on self-determination. It recognises that services are delivered most effectively if they are tailored to the conditions and cultures of specific communities. Community practice works at several levels and includes the work of community activists and self-managed groups as well as paid community workers and other professionals (Banks,

2003). It promotes social inclusion and participatory decision making involving service users, community members, statutory partners and other stakeholders. However, most community practitioners have their goals and targets set externally by employers or funders, rather than by the communities themselves. This is what makes it different from community development. Community practice is often located outside the main institutions, for example in a neighbourhood office or community-owned premises. It is a form of outreach or detached service delivery which aims to be more responsive than mainstream services to community needs and preferences.

Brief conclusion

Community development is sometimes described as a broad movement for social change. As can be seen from this chapter, in practice it takes many forms shaped by different ideologies. What they have in common is a commitment to working *with* people to remedy situations that are causing injustice, discontent or impoverishment. Despite its rather fuzzy nature as a profession, community development is regularly rediscovered, criticised and adapted by policy makers and governments seeking to achieve long-term improvements in the living conditions of communities that find themselves on the margins of civil society.

Summary

- Community development is about informal learning, collective action and organisational development.
- It is primarily concerned to support communities around issues that they identify for themselves but also works with public bodies to improve community engagement.

■ Community development aims to increase social justice and works to a number of core values, notably to promote equality, empowerment and cooperation.
■ It is useful to consider three different models of community development: radical, pluralist and communitarian.
■ As an approach, community development techniques can be adopted by other professions working with communities.

Further reading

There are a number of useful readers on community development, as well as practical guides on working with community groups and on community engagement strategies. The Community Development Foundation has a range of publications and the national occupational standards for community development work are available from the Federation for Community Development Learning. The Community Development Exchange website provides an update on current debates and lists many useful resources.

Henderson and Vercseg's (2010) exploration of how community development relates to civil society uses interesting examples from the UK and Eastern Europe. Alan Twelvetrees' latest edition of *Community work* (2008) is a basic text for practitioners and Margaret Ledwith has authored several thought-provoking books which take a more radical approach.

3
the changing context of community development

||||||||||||||||||||||||||||||||||||||||||||||||||||||||||||||||||||||||||||||||||||||||||||||||||||||||||||||||||||||||

This chapter begins by tracking the way in which community development has evolved over the years and the factors that have shaped this evolution. It then identifies the policy themes that have driven interest in community development and describes the contribution community development can make to these policy drivers: welfare and service reform; democratic renewal; restoring community; and regenerating places and economies.

How community policies have developed

Origins and early applications

Community development has many foundations in the past. Some can be found in communities themselves: the mutual organisations and friendly societies of the eighteenth and nineteenth centuries, for example, where, as industrialisation gained pace, working class people banded together to pool their resources and meet common needs. Others can be found in external initiatives. One example is the Settlement movement, mentioned in our introductory chapter, which began in the 1880s and brought middle and upper class volunteers into poor urban areas to work with local communities. Another can be found in colonial community development since World War II, introduced first to provide a bulwark against communism and to foster economic development in the interests of empire and later to prepare the indigenous population for a peaceful transition to independence. Marj Mayo (1975) traces similar 'colonial' antecedents in the US, where,

---

she argues, black self-help projects were encouraged in order to stave off discontent among the black and minority ethnic population and ensure a skilled and disciplined industrial labour force.

Other foundations lie in the housing and planning field. The origins of the tenants' movement, for example, lie in the early twentieth century with campaigns for social housing and rent strikes and the associations formed by tenants of the new local authority housing estates as the century progressed. By the 1950s, mass postwar slum clearance and physical redevelopment programmes were causing concern about the break-up of communities. The Institute for Community Studies, launched in 1954, compared the soullessness of the postwar New Towns and council estates unfavourably with the dense social ties of life in the East London slums from which inhabitants had been moved (Young and Willmott, 1962). Development workers were drafted into these new towns and estates to promote social activities and help build a sense of community (Goetschius, 1969).

The foundations of a more radical approach lie in the 1960s and 1970s, with the growth of the civil rights, peace and women's movements and growing unrest across the globe. Racial tensions flared in the US and in the UK, provoked in the latter case by the notorious 'Rivers of Blood' speech by Enoch Powell, a prominent Conservative MP. It was also becoming clear that, despite all the promise of the postwar welfare state, poverty and disadvantage had not been eliminated. In response, governments unleashed an arsenal of new social initiatives to regenerate 'deprived' areas: in the US, the War on Poverty, with its Community Action Program, Model Cities Program and the Special Impact Program in the mid-1960s; in the UK, the Urban Programme, the Comprehensive Community Programme and the National Community Development Project, towards the end of the decade.

Most of these new policy initiatives were to founder as the 1970s progressed (although the Urban Programme survived in various guises into the 1990s). In part, this was because of their internal contradictions – between the limited aspirations of government and the expectations raised in the populations targeted by these interventions. In part also, it was because they encountered fierce resistance from local politicians (for an analysis of 'what went wrong', see Marris and Rein, 1967, and Loney, 1983). Their demise was also hastened by the oil crisis of the early 1970s and the accompanying recession, which signalled the end of the postwar boom and eventually led to the rise of neoliberalism, with its ideology of shrinking the state in favour of the market. Community campaigns that had attacked public services now found they had to defend them (Craig et al, 2011). With the election of Ronald Reagan in the US and Margaret Thatcher in the UK, urban regeneration focused increasingly on local economic and physical revival in order to create jobs and stimulate industrial growth. In some quarters, state support for disadvantaged people was seen as encouraging dependency and the emergence of a 'moral underclass'.

Although community development had little place in this ideology, it continued to thrive in some areas. In the UK, for example, local authorities opposed to Margaret Thatcher's neoliberal ideology continued to support community development, while the emphasis on the consumer in the market, coupled with the desire to rein in local government, led to a succession of initiatives to engage service users in the design and planning of welfare services. Across the Atlantic, the community development corporations (CDCs) set up in the 1960s were to grow in number and size. But some US commentators suggest that, as federal funding dried up, CDCs became increasingly entrepreneurial, filling the vacuum left by the withdrawal of the state and receding further and further from their original goals (see, for example, De Filippis, 2007). By the end of the 1980s, an editorial in the international *Community Development Journal* was very pessimistic about the prospects for the future (Craig et al, 1990).

The renaissance of community

The 1990s, however, brought the beginnings of a revival. The Cities Challenge programme in the UK and the Empowerment Zones and Enterprise Communities (EZ/EC) in the US sought to increase economic investment, but began to emphasise again the need to involve communities in both the planning and delivery of regeneration programmes. In the UK, this was to be the start of a new wave of initiatives that culminated in 2001 with the National Strategy for Neighbourhood Renewal (NSNR), launched by the New Labour

---

Box 3.1   New Labour's National Strategy for Neighbourhood Renewal

The National Strategy for Neighbourhood Renewal was launched in 2001. It was based on an unprecedented and comprehensive consultation with communities, academics, practitioners and policy makers through 17 Policy Action Teams covering the many different facets of neighbourhood-based social exclusion. It drew in the New Deal for Communities (NDC) Programme, which had already been set up in 39 neighbourhoods, and set up a range of other initiatives, including a Neighbourhood Renewal Fund (NRF) targeted at the 88 most disadvantaged neighbourhoods, a Neighbourhood Wardens Programme in 84 neighbourhoods and Neighbourhood Management Pathfinders in 35 neighbourhoods. Its aim was to close the gap between the most disadvantaged neighbourhoods and the rest of society, focusing particularly on addressing worklessness, poor educational attainment, poor health, community safety, housing and the environment. It was intended as a long-term strategy – the NDCs were funded for ten years, Neighbourhood Management Pathfinders for seven. Meanwhile, a Single Community Programme was set up in each of the 88 NRF neighbourhoods to provide infrastructure support to local organisations. The programme involved a Community Chest and a Community Learning Chest; also, a Community Empowerment Fund to support the formation of Community Empowerment Networks to feed into local decision making. The Strategy also included the formation of a National Community Forum of experienced residents to advise government on neighbourhood renewal policy.

government in 2001. Parallel initiatives were established in the soon to be devolved administrations of Scotland, Northern Ireland and Wales.

The National Strategy's long-term vision of reducing inequalities between the most disadvantaged neighbourhoods and the rest of society faded later in the decade. But community empowerment moved into the mainstream, not only as a requirement of regeneration funding, but also as part of New Labour's Local Government Modernisation Agenda. 'Community' was no longer simply 'prescribed for the poor' (Taylor, 2011). It was for everyone. And, while the language may now be different, the emphasis on community has survived the change of government and ideology from New Labour to the Conservative-Liberal Democrat coalition formed after the 2010 election. Giving communities more say and more control is a core element of the coalition's flagship 'Big Society' agenda.

Interest in community development has not, of course, been confined to the US and the UK. Ironically, perhaps, given the criticism that their structural adjustment policies have attracted from community development commentators, community participation has been a feature of the development agendas of the International Monetary Fund and the World Bank. Their programmes often specify community participation, alongside devolution and privatisation, as a requirement for financial aid, with community development seen as a tool for democratic restructuring. Many international non-governmental organisations (NGOs) and aid agencies have also supported community development alongside the more immediate demands of disaster response, as a way of creating more sustainable responses to the challenges faced by such communities.

Policy and practice in the global South are increasingly influencing the North. There are three reasons for this: the influence of the popular education movement on radical practice, building on the praxis of Paulo Freire (1972; see also Chapter Two, this volume); a response to the democratic innovations that popular movements bring when they come to power, for example, participatory budgeting in Brazil; and a reflection of the fact that we now live in a globalised world, with significant opportunities for community development to learn across national and regional barriers (Mayo, 2005). We could, of course, argue that globalisation is nothing new. We referred earlier to the roots of community development in colonialism and its role in supporting imperial economies. But with the hollowing out of the nation state and the revolution in internet-based communication, the implications for community development are now very different. Information technology has given local communities unprecedented access to data and knowledge, allowing them to network, compare experience and take collective action on a global scale.

Community development policy and practice are also influenced by another aspect of globalisation, and that is the increasing movement of people across state borders, sometimes willingly but often unwillingly. This affects communities in many different ways. Many community workers have grappled with issues of immigration, particularly the need to tackle the tensions that arise as 'host' communities close ranks against newcomers, defining themselves by who they are *not* as much as who they are. Racial tensions have been a major trigger for community development initiatives in different parts of the world, and community cohesion was a major government priority of the later New Labour years in the UK.

This brief history of the evolution of community development demonstrates the durability of 'community' and community participation across ideological divides. The UK coalition government's Big Society agenda, for example, sees community as the alternative to 'big government'. It aims to give citizens and communities more powers; encourage people to take on active roles and responsibilities in civil society; transfer power down to local level; and support co-ops, mutuals and social enterprises. The government also states its intention to: 'train a new generation of community organisers and support the creation of neighbourhood groups across the UK, especially in the most deprived areas' (Cabinet Office, 2010).

The UK Prime Minister, David Cameron, who has driven the Big Society vision, has moved a long way from his Conservative predecessor,

Margaret Thatcher, who famously proclaimed that there was no such thing as society. Communities are clearly central to his thinking. So what is the enduring appeal of community, over time and across the ideological divide? In the rest of this chapter, we consider four overlapping drivers of the interest in community development over recent years:

- welfare and service reform in the face of both growing need and ideological change;
- democratic renewal in the face of falling voting figures and disillusionment with formal politics;
- restoring community in the face of perceived moral breakdown and fragmentation;
- regenerating places and economies in the face of economic change and abandonment.

Welfare and service reform

The policy preference for at least three decades now has been to reduce the role of the state and introduce markets into welfare through different forms of privatisation. Governments have also brought in policies to give communities and service users a greater say in the design and delivery of public services, from environmental services to schools, policing and health. In the UK, 'community' posts have been established within many services, to support consultation, improve information and bring services closer to their users both psychologically and physically. Neighbourhood management models have been introduced to join up services in a way that makes more sense to residents and better serves their needs. Over recent years, there has been increasing emphasis, too, on giving communities the chance to run their own services. This has been most prevalent in the field of housing, with the promotion of tenant management and control since the 1990s, but is set to accelerate with proposals to give communities new powers to save local facilities and services threatened with closure and to take over state-run services.

Critics claim that these proposals are a mask for the savage cuts in public expenditure that are being made by the coalition government, cuts which are expected to hit the poorest communities particularly hard (Browne and Levell, 2010). They argue that opportunities for communities to take over services are in any case more likely to appeal to the better off than people in low income neighbourhoods. The most likely outcome of transferring service delivery away from the state will probably be increased provision by larger private companies and the professional voluntary sector. If this is the case, despite government commitment to localism, services may be run by national concerns, with less local accountability.

It would be a mistake to see a move to community-run services solely as an external imposition, however. Many people in the most disadvantaged communities have suffered over the years from poor facilities and inadequate and stigmatising services with high staff turnover. There is no shortage of examples where residents have successfully run their own services and facilities (Wind-Cowie, 2010). In addition, communities have always provided more informal support and services to their members. With rising levels of need, this will continue.

So what are the implications of these trends for community development? It clearly has a vital contribution to offer in supporting those who do want to take advantage of the new opportunities to run services and manage assets and ensure that they are adequately resourced to do so. However, there are many who simply want 'decent' and responsive services without having to run them themselves. In this context, community development has a particular role to play in helping residents to defend the services that they need and to hold providers to account. Either way, it can play a part in ensuring that services and facilities, whoever runs them, are accessible, equitable and accountable.

Democratic renewal

As world institutions seek to extend democracy across the world, voting figures in the more established democracies have been falling for decades at national and local level. The membership of mass political parties has declined as well – by more than three quarters since 1964 in the UK. Here and elsewhere, the public appears to have become increasingly disillusioned with formal politics.

There are a variety of reasons for this, from small- and large-scale political corruption to the changing circumstances of contemporary life. Mass institutions no longer have the appeal they once did; people are more likely to be interested in single-issue politics. Governing elites seem more and more distant from the man or woman on the street. In the UK, for example, the national politician who has made his or her way up through local government or even a 'real job' seems an increasing rarity. The mass media have changed the nature of politics too. All these factors have created a crisis of legitimacy for representative democracy.

At the same time, the complexity of society and the limitations on the capacity of any state – however well run – to meet the needs of its citizens has prompted a well-documented shift from 'government' to more participative forms of 'governance', with the growth of partnership working (see Chapter Four). The language of citizen participation is everywhere, promoted by supranational institutions like the World Bank and the European Union (EU), as well as national governments around the world. The EU, for example has made the promotion of participatory democracy a key objective and introduced a Citizens' Initiative that allows one million citizens from a number of member states to call on the Commission to bring forward new policy proposals. It has also set up a Citizens' Agora, which brings citizens, civil society organisations and elected politicians together to debate key challenges for the EU.

National and local governments have introduced new partnership and participatory mechanisms and there is a thirst for innovatory methods of deliberative democracy, as the spread of participatory budgeting from its Brazilian heartland demonstrates. In the UK, the New Labour government committed itself to modernising local government and introduced a range of legislative reforms to give citizens a greater voice, from a 'Duty To Involve' to provisions for a 'community call to action'. Participation was also included in the set of national indicators it introduced as part of the settlement between central and local government, with a measure of the 'percentage of people who feel they can influence decisions in their locality'. Programmes were introduced to support community empowerment and 'active citizenship', working both with local government and with communities to build commitment and capacity.

At local level, citizen participation can only work if there is something meaningful to influence. Devolution is therefore an important part of the discourse, again promoted globally by the World Bank and through successive layers of government. Thus, in 2005, David Miliband, then the first Minister of Communities and Local Government in the UK, made 'double devolution' part of his platform – to local government and beyond that to the citizen and the individual. The current government has also committed itself to the 'radical devolution of power and greater financial autonomy to locally governed bodies, including a full review of local government finance' (Cabinet Office, 2010).

In this context, it will be vital that the potential for engagement and influence is extended to all citizens and includes those whose voices are seldom heard. Of course, community voice does not depend solely on the opportunities provided by power holders – the 'invited spaces' that government and others provide (Cornwall, 2004). Independent community action has a long tradition of its own, with communities running their own campaigns and claiming their own 'popular spaces' for change (see Chapter Four for a fuller discussion). These provide a strong base from which to engage with government if communities choose to do so. However, many of the more traditional working class organisations where citizens found a common voice, gained a political education and established their collective strength, have disappeared. Political parties, trade unions, adult education institutes and social clubs, for example, no longer have a presence in many local neighbourhoods, nor are they able to inspire solidarity beyond their membership.

Community development has long supported those who do not have a voice in taking collective action. It has an important role to play, too, in cultivating new 'popular spaces' to replace – or revive – those that have gone, creating opportunities for dialogue and debate which can encourage political awareness and confidence among the most disadvantaged citizens. It can link communities with a common cause and engage community representatives in more formal governance structures, so that local action can be influential at the levels where key decisions are made. At the same time, it needs to work with external actors – public or private – to raise their awareness and capacity to engage with communities.

Restoring community

'Community lost' has been a strong theme of social commentary at least since the industrial revolution, and this concern has been reflected in policy debates. In the 1990s, a strong communitarian tradition emerged based in part on a perceived breakdown in moral cohesion and responsibility and the loss of 'social capital', a concept popularised by Robert Putnam (1993) to describe the networks, norms and trust that underpin community and collective action (for further discussion, see Chapter Four). Some blamed this breakdown on the dependency created by state welfare; others saw the individualism of the market as the villain of the piece, giving rise to increasing fragmentation and the 'death of the social' (Rose, 1996). The theme of a 'broken society' has been a favourite of politicians over the centuries and persists to the present day, regardless of the evidence.

Other factors threaten traditional notions of community. The movement of people across the globe is accompanied by racial tension; the ageing of the population risks intergenerational tension. The diversity of cultures raises questions as to whether it is realistic any more to talk about a shared identity or a common moral compass. As we shall explore further in Chapter Seven, communities are increasingly made up of people with multiple allegiances and divergent cultures.

The current economic crisis could have a devastating effect on areas that have already lost the industries that shaped them and will now be hardest hit by the impact of public spending cuts on jobs and services (Browne and Levell, 2010). There is much talk now about the need for 'community resilience', the capacity of communities to adapt to change and recover from crises such as the impact of a natural disaster or the effects of the recession.

Robert Putnam's argument about social capital, which resonated strongly with policy makers throughout the world, was that it underpinned democracy. It has since been linked with a range of other positive outcomes (Halpern, 2005; see also Chapter Four, this volume). 'Restoring community' can thus be seen as the foundation stone to the other policy themes discussed here. Without basic community development at local level, other interventions are unlikely to be adequately rooted. However, this should not obscure the need for policies that address the structural and economic factors that marginalise significant sections of the population.

Over the years there have been numerous policy strands designed to 'restore community'. Civil renewal and 'active citizenship' initiatives seek to support volunteering, self-help and neighbourliness, encouraging people to look out for one other, promoting 'resilience' and 'bonding' social capital. These tend to be a constant whatever the ideological persuasion of government. 'Community cohesion' and similar policies seek to connect communities and facilitate 'meaningful interactions' that build bridging social capital across races, faiths, generations and other potential fault lines. Concern with the rise of the far right in Europe has also led to debate about the alienation of the white working class and to the introduction of programmes to tackle this.

Again, it is important to recognise that communities do not wait for state initiatives to bring them together informally and formally. This is the stuff of everyday community action. But in fractured and neglected neighbourhoods, where social bonds have been eroded by factors far outside the residents' control, or in neighbourhoods where individual and family survival takes up enormous amounts of energy, community development has an important role in supporting this basic activity and reducing isolation and suspicion.

Regenerating places and economies

Poverty is not confined to particular localities. However, it *is* concentrated in particular neighbourhoods – often in areas of public housing. These neighbourhoods – the ones that economic changes have left behind – were the focus of the 1960s initiatives discussed earlier in this chapter.

Often the focus in regeneration initiatives is primarily on regenerating local economies so that they become 'working neighbourhoods', with an emphasis on job creation and community economic development. Or they have focused on housing redevelopment. But like the War on Poverty and the Community Development Projects, programmes such as the more recent National Strategy for Neighbourhood Renewal in the UK (which a later Working Neighbourhoods Fund largely replaced) have taken a much more comprehensive approach, tackling worklessness, health inequalities, poor educational attainment, environmental decay and crime (see Box 3.1).

Community development has, of course, had a close relationship with planning and housing policy – both in disadvantaged areas and more generally. Recent policy emphasis on place shaping in the UK has adopted a holistic approach, while the new UK coalition government's Big Society includes plans to reform the planning system to 'give neighbourhoods far more ability to determine the shape of the places in which their inhabitants live'. Community development has also had a role to play to support communities in opposing plans which have gone against the wishes of the community. Plans to demolish housing which residents felt should be rehabilitated were common in the 1970s, for example, and one of the most famous campaigns was in the Coin Street area just next to London's South Bank, where local residents successfully and with the eventual support of the Greater London Council – fought off plans to demolish their homes to make way for offices. This campaign has since grown into a highly successful community enterprise, turning over millions of pounds and providing accommodation for homes, shops, offices and entertainment facilities.

Current policy promotes the transfer of assets – buildings, public spaces and so on – to communities alongside the development of local social enterprises. Both strategies help people to gain a sense of place, in preserving local heritage or identity and in regenerating local economies. We referred earlier to the highly successful community development corporation movement in the US. While slower to take off in England, community ownership and management of assets has grown appreciably over the past ten years or so, partly as the result of 'endowments' from major regeneration initiatives which transfer the ownership of social housing to tenant management organisations, partly through the enterprise of residents themselves, partly through community economic development initiatives. Governments the world over are also promoting forms of 'social innovation' that can combine social with commercial goals and achieve the 'double' or even 'triple' bottom line (economic, social and environmental). There is, of course a strong and innovative community economic development tradition to learn from in the global South, as well as the social economy tradition in Europe, built on the principles of mutuality and solidarity that characterised the early friendly societies with which we began this chapter.

Brief conclusion

Community development has a long history in public policy and practice as part of the wider and longstanding interest in community. Successive governments across the world have sought to strengthen community ties, build community capacity and resilience and 'restore community'. Communities have been seen as a critical resource in policies to reform services, to revitalise democracy and to regenerate local environments and economies. Community development can support communities to make full use of these opportunities, while ensuring that they meet real community needs. It also has an important role to play in building links with policy makers and other external actors to ensure that opportunities are developed in dialogue with communities and supported by policies that address the wider causes of exclusion and inequality.

Summary

- Community development has come in and out of fashion as policies change, but since the beginning of the 1990s, 'community' and community participation have been promoted by international institutions as well as national governments.
- Community development has been influenced by popular movements, from the civil rights movement of the 1960s to global campaigns in the twenty-first century.
- One driver for the policy interest in community development has been the desire to roll back the state and to give service users a greater say in welfare provision.
- Community development has also been promoted as part of the drive to address the democratic deficit, through increased citizen and community participation and through devolving powers from central government.
- A third factor has been concern over the fragmentation of community life and the perceived loss of 'social capital', which is blamed both on the growth of the state and the individualism associated with the market.
- Community development has a central role to play in the regeneration of neighbourhoods that have suffered from the collapse of traditional industry and the increasing spatial concentration of poverty.

Further reading

Most books on community development provide a historical account. Students will find the community development readers that have been produced in this country and the US particularly useful in this respect (de Filippis and Saegert (2007)*The community development reader*; Craig et al (2011) *Community development in the United Kingdom 1950–2010*; Craig et al (2008) *Community development in theory and practice*). Those who are interested in learning from history (rather than repeating it) will find much of interest in the classic texts by Peter Marris and Martin Rein (1967) on the war on poverty and Martin Loney (1983) on the National Community Development Project.

4

theoretical concepts

This chapter examines some of the theoretical perspectives and concepts that can inform community development, its understanding of the context within which it works and the potential for social change. It will focus on theories of: community, social capital and collective efficacy; the state, democracy and power; institutional and complexity theory; and social movement theory.

Community development has values – primarily of social justice and democracy, for example – but these tell us what it is trying to achieve, not how it might do so. Theories help us to understand why and how facts and events come to be as they are and provide an analytical framework to guide our judgements and actions.

Theories from a variety of different disciplines can inform community development by helping to explain the world in which it intervenes, and community workers may use a variety of different theories of change to decide on strategies and which model of practice to pursue. There are theories that help to explain how communities work (or not); how power works; how policies are made; how people can be mobilised and what motivates them; how collective action can be organised; and how systems operate and adjust to change. There are theories of 'social change', of democracy, of the state. There are also theories of civil society, associations, relationships and networks. Economic, sociological, psychological and management theories all have something to offer to our understanding of community and community development.

—

43

Finding a way through this wide array of theoretical approaches is a lifetime's work. Certainly, in a book of this size, it is impossible to cover – let alone do justice to – all the theories that may prove useful to the student or practitioner of community development. So in this chapter we set out some of the key ideas that we have found most useful, offering a brief guide and some signposts to further reading. In other chapters we have developed theory about practice itself, which is sometimes known as praxis. We start by exploring the concept of community and associated theories of social capital and collective efficacy. We move on to theories of the state and of democracy, since these are the context within which community development operates. The next section broadens the discussion out to consider theories of power and what they can tell us about the relationship between 'structure' and 'agency', that is, how much of what communities do and experience is determined for them and how much they can determine for themselves. We then briefly consider how a fourth family of theories – about systems and institutions – help us to understand more about the structures that promote or prevent change. In our final section we visit some aspects of social movement theory, to learn about opportunities for change and how to mobilise people for collective action. In each section, we highlight the implications for community development.

Theories of community

'Community' can mean many different things. One study in the mid-twentieth century (Hillery, 1955) found 94 definitions of community, and the most that could be agreed on was that community involves social interaction and some ties or bonds in common. Community can simply be a description – of a group or network of people who have something in common. Or it can be used normatively to suggest certain values indicating how communities *should* operate, for example, with community as a site of moral cohesion, where people trust each other and are prepared to help each other out. It can also be used instrumentally to suggest agency, implying that communities can act together to achieve common ends or implement government policies

(Butcher et al, 1993; Taylor, 2011). While some might search for a definition of community that is free from normative and instrumental connotations, however, in a seminal book in 1974 (pp 10, 12), Raymond Plant argued that we should not be preoccupied with looking at the language of community in a one-dimensional way, but be more alive to the 'open texture' of its use – 'its actual use in language and thought, in the description, interpretation, organisation and evaluation of behaviour'. He went on to claim that: '[c]ommunity is so much part of the stock in trade of social and political argument that it is unlikely that some non-ambiguous and non-contested definition of the notion can be given'.

In his book, Plant tracks interest in community back to German sociological thought in the late eighteenth and early nineteenth centuries. This in turn referred back to the ideal of the Greek *polis*: whose culture was regarded as homogeneous, participatory and open to all (meaning, at that time, all free men). This notion of community contrasted the 'whole man' with the more fragmented forms of functional interaction typical of modern mass society. These concerns were captured in the distinction that Ferdinand Tönnies made in the late nineteenth century between *Gemeinschaft* and *Gesellschaft*, which contrasted traditional organic, territorial communities (often seen as rural) with the newer fragmented, contractual relationships that characterised industrialised urban society.

The ties of community were also contrasted with the impersonality of the state. Robert Nisbet (1953), for example, drew on nineteenth century German traditions to argue for the importance of community as a critical mediating institution between state and citizen (see also Plant, 1974). Others have seen 'community' as an *alternative* to the state, a view promoted in the 1990s by the communitarian movement, referred to in previous chapters. Spearheaded by Amitai Etzioni, communitarianism became influential in many policy circles at the time, offering 'a political vocabulary which eschews market individualism, but not capitalism; and which embraces collective action, but not class or the state' (Driver and Martell, 1997, p 33). Strongly normative, it emphasises respect for others as well as self-respect, responsibilities as well as rights, self-government and service to others, with the family first and then the community as the sites in which moral norms and obligations are developed (Etzioni, 1998). As we saw earlier, the communitarian influence remains evident today in the concept of the Big Society, with its emphasis on communities organising things for themselves without hindrance from government officials or state monitoring.

The early 1990s also saw the introduction of another highly influential concept into the community portfolio. 'Social capital' – a concept that we have already encountered in earlier chapters – can trace its roots back to the early twentieth century, but was introduced into popular debate in the 1990s through the work of Robert Putnam, who defined it as 'features of social life – network, norms and trust – that enable participants to act together more effectively to pursue shared objectives' (Putnam, 1993, pp 664–5). Putnam highlighted the importance of relationships of trust in making democracy work, seeing social capital as a moral resource and lamenting its decline in the US. The World Bank reflected this view, referring in 1999 to social capital as the 'glue' that holds the institutions that underpin a society together. As a resource, high levels of social capital have been linked with greater productivity, effective democracy, better, safer communities, higher educational achievement and a host of other positive effects (see, for example, Halpern, 2005).

Some theorists, including Putnam and James Coleman (1990), define social capital as a collective resource on which individuals can draw. Portes (1995, p 12), on the other hand defines it as an individual resource: 'the capacity of individuals to command scarce resources by virtue of their membership in networks or broader social structures'. In this, he draws on the work of Pierre Bourdieu, who identified social capital as a third form of capital alongside economic and cultural capital.

Like 'community', social capital is a contested term, capable of many interpretations. Bourdieu argued that, as an individual resource, social capital was as inequitably distributed as any other form of capital, thus reinforcing existing divisions and privileges in society (Bourdieu, 1986).

Later commentators have criticised the tendency of social capital's champions to confuse the definition of social capital with the positive outcomes it is supposed to deliver. Networks, norms and trust can be exclusive, secretive and unaccountable. Close ties can be oppressive, and facilitate social stagnation and resistance to change (Burns and Taylor, 1998; Sampson, 2004).

Some of these concerns have been addressed by the distinctions that Michael Woolcock (1998) and others have made between different forms of social capital: bonding, bridging and linking:

- Bonding social capital describes enduring strong relations between people in similar situations, such as close friends and family.
- Bridging social capital describes weaker, more boundary spanning connections between different people, or different ethnic or geographical communities.
- Linking social capital describes connections between people that cut across status and link people with differing levels of power, service users and service providers, for example, or community members and government officials.

While bonding social capital is good for 'getting by', bridging and linking social capital are needed for 'getting ahead'. The distinction between bonding and bridging builds on work by Mark Granovetter (1973), who argued that, when it came to seeking employment, strong ties were less effective than a large and more diverse network of weaker ties. Similarly, Wellman (1979) has argued that, while weaker ties may have limits in terms of the claims that can be made on them, they can provide indirect access to a greater diversity of resources than can stronger, more socially homogeneous ties.

So what does this mean for community development? The distinction between different forms of capital is particularly important in community development, for social change cannot be achieved simply by working at community level on small-scale projects or local campaigns. Bridging and linking social capital are needed to harness resources and influence beyond the community, to connect with allies and broader social movements (Ledwith and Springett, 2010). And while many disadvantaged communities are characterised by strong ties (they can 'get by'), they are often poorly connected with those outside their boundaries, whether other communities or power holders, whose resources they need to help them to 'get ahead'. Community development, therefore, needs to build relationships and trust within and between communities as well as with power holders in order to identify and act on common interests.

But what will translate these ties into action? To answer this question, we need to take a brief step sideways into questions of individual motivation and collective efficacy.

Understanding motivation and efficacy

Behaviourist models of motivation argue that people's behaviour can be explained as a rational strategy to maximise personal benefits and minimise costs in response to patterns of probable rewards and incentives. However, this is widely criticised as too simplistic and ignoring the complexity of factors that affect motivation. One theory with which most community development workers will be familiar is that of Abraham Maslow (1943). He argues that there is a hierarchy of needs that starts with basic physiological requirements, and then moves through security and safety, belongingness, self-esteem and recognition, to self-actualisation. Self-actualisation, he argues, is only attainable if the layers of need below it in this hierarchy have been satisfied.

Albert Bandura's theory of self-efficacy explores further the factors that determine how people motivate themselves and behave in specific situations. He defines self-efficacy as people's beliefs about their capabilities to behave in such a way that will 'exercise influence over events that affect their lives' (Bandura, 1994, p 1). He argues that these beliefs are the result of social processes and have four main sources:

- experience (success increases self-efficacy; failure lowers it);
- social modelling (if s/he can do it, so can I);

- social persuasion (encouragement not only in terms of positive appraisals but also in structuring situations in which people are likely to succeed);
- physical and emotional factors and how they are perceived.

It is easy to see from this list how the circumstances in people's lives undermine their self-efficacy and sense of belonging. People will be less likely to engage in any kind of collective action if their life experience does not instil confidence in their ability to succeed, if they have few models of success around them, if they are rarely encouraged or put in a situation where they can succeed and if engaging in any kind of public action makes them feel anxious, angry or insecure (Taylor, 2011).

The concept of collective efficacy, as developed by Robert Sampson and others in their research on crime prevention (Sampson et al, 2002; Sampson, 2004), is rooted in self-efficacy. But Sampson is critical of policies that focus on the individual. In this he is in agreement with social capital theory, stressing the importance of personal ties, cooperation and social interaction. A study in Chicago carried out over several years (Sampson et al, 2002) observed that the neighbourhoods which seemed to have low rates of vandalism and less serious crime were those where residents appeared to have strong social networks and a belief that by working together they could make things happen. The study found more social interaction on the streets in these areas, and evidence of community-level organisations working to improve the neighbourhood.

Networks are only part of the explanation for collective efficacy, however. Sampson's research focuses on the conditions that link interpersonal ties and trust with shared expectations for action. 'Networks', he argues, 'are differentially invoked; and, in fact dense tight-knit networks may actually impede social organisation, if they are isolated or weakly linked to collective expectations for action' (2007, p 168). They 'have to be activated to be ... meaningful' (2004, p 108). He underlines the importance of 'a strong institutional infrastructure', where the legitimacy of social order comes in part from mutual engagement and negotiation among residents, mediating institutions and agencies of law enforcement (p 113), emphasising what social capital theorists would call linking as well as bonding and bridging ties. As part of this infrastructure, his research stresses not only the importance of participation in grassroots community organisations but also the presence of neighbourhood services. Sampson is critical of policies that undermine trust, including zero tolerance and mass imprisonment. He also emphasises the negative impact of structural inequality on collective efficacy. 'Inequality in resources', he argues, 'matters greatly for explaining the production of collective efficacy' (2004).

The relevance of community development in promoting self- and collective efficacy is clear. Community workers can help to create Bandura's conditions for self-efficacy by giving people the opportunity for positive experiences of engagement that will build their confidence, by helping them identify the factors that led to success or failure, by putting them in touch with groups which have been successful, by offering encouragement, and by giving them opportunities to discuss how they feel about experiences of success or failure. They can also build the links between communities and external organisations that Sampson identifies as essential to social stability and local control (Sampson, 2007, p 169). But as Sampson argues, efficacy does not just depend on the conditions people create for themselves. To understand more about the relationship between disadvantaged communities and external players, we need now to consider theories of the state.

Theories of the state

Much community development in the immediate postwar era in the UK operated on the basis of encouraging people in disadvantaged neighbourhoods to build 'community' and to help themselves. It also worked with local service providers to make them more responsive to need. But, as we saw in Chapter Three, this approach was rejected in the 1970s by workers in the UK Community Development Projects (CDPs), who described it as 'gilding the ghetto'. They placed the responsibility for the plight of disadvantaged communities not with the community but with the state as the instrument of capitalism, highlighting the flight of financial capital from these areas and describing how state subsidy, for example in housing policy, favoured the middle classes – a critique paralleled in the US (see, for example, O'Connor, 2007).

The CDP critique was grounded in Marxist theory, which argues that the political and cultural arrangements in any given society are determined by the relationships of production and that the state is the instrument of the capitalist class. But Marx argued that capitalism contained inherent contradictions. Because the economic cycles of capitalism inevitably generate conflict between the classes, Marx argued that capitalism contained the seeds of its own destruction. Change would come when the oppressed class rose up against the bourgeoisie and placed the means of production under collective ownership, allowing the state to wither away.

Box 4.1 Marxist theory

In its classic form, Marxism argues that, under capitalism, society is ruled by those who control the means of production (the owners of factories, mills, land and agricultural equipment, for example). The state is defined as the instrument of the capitalist class and the political and cultural arrangements in any given society are determined by the relationships of production. Marxism explains the class system in terms of the labour employed under capitalism, which creates surplus value (profit), making it possible for the capitalists (the bourgeoisie) to live off the work of others (the proletariat). Marxist theory argues that capitalism alienates people from their work and generates a 'false consciousness' among the masses that leads them to act against their own best interests. Marx saw the fragmentation of society as part and parcel of industrial capitalism, which replaced the communal virtues of cooperation and solidarity with those of conflict and competition.

The collapse of communism in the 1990s challenged the Marxist analysis, and some of the most influential theory over the years was to come instead from other thinkers in the Marxist stable, notably Antonio Gramsci and Paulo Freire. Gramsci, for example, was critical of Marxist economic determinism and focused instead on the ideological apparatus of the capitalist state. He introduced the idea of 'hegemony' to explain how dominant ideologies pervade society and become accepted as common sense:

> Whereas coercion is exercised overtly through the armed forces, the police, the courts and the prisons, consent is subtly woven in through the institutions of civil society – the family, schools, the media, political parties, religious organisations, cultural, charitable and community groups – in a way that permeates our social being and asserts hegemonic control by influencing our ideas. (Ledwith, 1997, pp 122–3)

Marxism is one of a set of theories that argues that power is held by certain fixed groups or forces in society. In particular, it characterises society as based on class conflict, with different sections inextricably caught up in opposition due to their competing interests. Other 'conflict' models include theories of elite domination, patriarchy and structural racism. A further group of theories, while less conflictual, has explored the way in which actors within the state maximise their own interests – these range from public choice theory to theories of bureaucracy.

Community groups on their own are unlikely to have the resources or institutional capacity to counter these dominant forces. As indicated in Chapter Two, therefore, radical models of community development have promoted strategic alliances between disadvantaged communities and the labour movement. Community development has also turned to the critical dialogue models of Gramsci and Freire as a means of raising the consciousness of the powerless in order to challenge existing hegemonies and forms of systemic power. Instead of Marxist revolution, Gramsci saw change as coming through education, cultural shifts and the formation of social movements. He argued that critical consciousness is developed through praxis and informed dialogue, ideas that were to be developed by Paulo Freire in Latin America through an approach termed 'critical pedagogy'. To Freire, as we saw in Chapter Two, this was an educative process that allowed 'the oppressed' to reflect on their experience and question ideas and situations that they previously took for granted. This was a 'guided' process involving facilitators and experts who encouraged learning and debate. Gramsci, for example saw the importance of outside 'educators' as catalysts for change – but he argued that change also required organic intellectuals, who remain culturally rooted in communities, combining knowledge and ideas with direct experience of class oppression (Ledwith, 2005, pp 123–5).

Pluralist theories of the state challenge the fixed and deterministic view adopted by conflict theories. They analyse power as something that is dispersed throughout society, with democratic decision making based on bargaining between different interests. A pluralist analysis sees the state as setting standards and upholding rights that protect the freedom of groups to further their political interests while preventing any one group from undermining the freedom of others. The overlapping nature of citizen interests, the pluralists argue, helps to ensure cohesion and prevents any one faction from dominating. In addition, different groups hold power in different policy arenas, and this, they argue, prevents power from gravitating to elites. In this view, as Chapter Two argues, the role of community development is to support disadvantaged communities in making their voices heard and in becoming politically active, to increase their bargaining power in relation to external forces.

Traditional pluralism has been criticised for its failure to acknowledge the imbalance of power between different interests in society or indeed to recognise tendencies towards oligarchy, whereby decision making remains with the few. Even corporatist forms of government, which formally incorporate potentially competing interests (such as class, business and labour, or different ethnic or religious groups) into the policy making process, are prone to elitism as well as privileging certain interests over others. Pluralist theory also fails to acknowledge the way that dominant hegemonics structure the operation of power. Jürgen Habermas, for example, is critical of the dominance of 'instrumental rationality' in society (Habermas, 1984). He argues for new forms of 'communicative action' which can confront the distortion of reality by the powerful and transform power relationships. But radical pluralists, like Chantal Mouffe and Ernst Laclau, are critical of Habermas too, arguing that rational agreement is impossible (Laclau and Mouffe, 1985; Mouffe, 2005). They reject deliberative forms of democracy and consensus politics, highlighting instead the necessity for what they call 'agonistic' forms of democracy, which can confront and work with difference.

There are a number of implications for community development here. It can work with communities to develop their confidence and voice, so that they can engage effectively, create their own narratives and challenge dominant hegemonies. It can work with power holders to develop opportunities for dialogue and build their capacity to engage in effective and more equal dialogue with communities. It can also help to create opportunities where disagreements can be expressed and differences confronted.

Governance and regime theorists also adopt a pluralist approach. They argue that, in today's complex and fragmented society, it is not possible for the state to govern on its own. Instead regimes are formed which bring new resources and knowledge into decision making circles. While regimes can still be relatively closed, the governance discourse highlights the potential for government to 'steer' and enable and to open its decision making up to greater participation and more widespread deliberation. In this way, Gerry Stoker has argued, governance networks involve not just influencing policy but taking over the business of government (Stoker, 1998, p 23). However, critics argue that the networks of governance, like any other networks, can be exclusive, opaque and unaccountable. The structure of society still privileges certain actors over others.

The literature on policy networks, however, suggests that there are different kinds of networks in the governance process, not all of which are closed. Marsh and Rhodes (1992), for example, distinguish between policy communities and issue networks, the former more exclusive, with closer working relations, a consistency of values and a balance of power, the latter looser and more diverse. Sabatier (1988) argues that the policy subsystem is composed of a number of 'advocacy coalitions' which compete for influence and for the attention of 'policy brokers'. While these coalitions are unlikely to influence the core beliefs of governing regimes, they can influence the way in which problems are framed and the detail of how to achieve common goals. Thus, the increasing interest shown by the state in community and community participation could be seen to give more disadvantaged groups an entrée into policy making circles, bringing knowledge, legitimacy and access to groups whose voices are seldom heard.

There is a further body of literature that analyses the ambiguity within the policy making process and the potential for failure at different points in the policy chain. Policy making has been described as a 'garbage can' or as a 'game' that, even if it ultimately serves the interests of capital, is difficult to keep fully under control.

This range of theory suggests that there are opportunities for communities and those who work with them to influence the policy game to their advantage and to have 'agency', a possibility to which we shall return in our next section on 'power'. If these opportunities are to be grasped, however, community development workers need to understand the dynamics of policy making, help groups to gain access to policy makers, and create alliances within and outwith the system.

Theories of power: structure or agency?

Community development has been defined as 'a long-term value based process which aims to address imbalances in power and bring about change founded on social justice, equality and inclusion' (FCDL, 2009a). An understanding of power is therefore critical to effective practice, understanding the different ways in which power is denied to communities, but also the potential for communities to generate their own forms of power and to shape the way power operates.

How power works

Many of the theories of the state we have discussed earlier assume that power is a zero-sum commodity – that the only way in which the powerless can gain power is to take it away from those who have it. Theorists in this school have also traced the different ways in which power can be manifested. Steven Lukes (2005), for example, identifies three dimensions of power. The first is where the powerful can directly dictate the actions of others; in the second, the powerful set the agenda or the terms on which the less powerful operate – Bachrach and Baratz (1962) call this the 'mobilisation of bias'. The third describes the situation where the powerless internalise and take for granted the assumptions of the powerful about what is and is not possible – the power over ideas, akin to Gramsci's concept of hegemony.

A zero-sum analysis of power focuses on who has 'power over' whom and how that power is exercised. There are alternative approaches that analyse power as more fluid, as more diffuse and as something that can be generated and reproduced – as 'power to'. These approaches are concerned with the question of how power is produced and what it is that releases people's capabilities or power to act. Potentially, theorists in this school see power as a positive-sum game, although much of the analysis still focuses on the ways in which power and knowledge are manipulated in order to encourage the oppressed to see their interests as identical to those of the oppressor.

Much of this thinking draws on the work of Michel Foucault. His early work explored the way in which mechanisms of knowledge and power shape or 'discipline' the 'subject', using increasingly sophisticated technologies of surveillance to create, classify and control society (Rabinow, 1984). While his analysis focuses on power as domination, however, Foucault's account does not see particular interests as possessing power – whether they be elites, classes or the state. Instead, he emphasises the 'capillary' nature of power and the way it operates *through* rather than *on* people. Central to his work is the argument that the exercise of power requires the compliance of willing subjects and his exploration of how this compliance is secured. He emphasises in particular the significance of discourse as a vehicle through which knowledge and power are transmitted.

Foucault's ideas have been taken up by the 'governmentality' school, which explores the way in which governing has become detached from government and is increasingly taking place 'at a distance from' the state. In this view, governing has become a domain of strategies, techniques and procedures through which different forces and groups in society attempt to render their programme operable (Rose and Miller, 1992). They explore the complex and subtle diffusion of techniques and forms of knowledge through which communities 'can be mobilised, enrolled, deployed in novel programmes' (Rose, 1999, p 176), 'acting as their own overseers, while believing themselves ... to be free of power, making their own choices, pursuing their own interests, assessing arguments rationally and coming to their own conclusions' (Lukes, 2005, p 106). In this way, governmentality theorists argue that communities govern themselves more effectively than the state ever could. This kind of governing also makes communities themselves responsible for resolving problems which are often beyond their control – and easy to blame if they fail.

Foucault's writings about power have been taken to mean that there is no avoiding domination, that it is 'everywhere' and there is no freedom from it or reasoning independent of it (Lukes, 2005, p 12). Indeed, Foucault's successors have often argued that, although the new emphasis on 'governance' rather than government is taken to mean that governing is happening 'at a distance from the state', this is an illusion. In fact, they argue, the state is acting as an instrument of the neoliberal agenda, and its power continues to operate in these new governance spaces – much as Lukes' third face of power suggests.

This analysis – and particularly Foucault's emphasis on discourse – reflects Gramsci's view of civil society as the site where consent is engineered in societies, ensuring the cultural ascendancy of the ruling class and capitalism's stability (Lukes, 2005, p 144). But Gramsci also sees civil society as the arena where hegemonic ideas of neoliberalism can be contested. In a similar vein, Foucault acknowledged that power could only be exercised over free subjects and therefore by its nature implies resistance: 'Just as discourses are diffused throughout society and power is everywhere, so too can resistance be encountered at every point, in attempts to evade, subvert or contest strategies of power' (Gaventa, 2003, p 2).

Translated into the current context, then, governmentality allows us to interpret neoliberalism not simply as an ideology or a political philosophy, but rather as an assemblage of techniques and technologies that facilitate the process of governing. This can then be interpreted negatively or positively: on the one hand tracing the advance of the neo-liberal agenda through multiple capillaries and agencies; more positively by recognising the multiple sites through which power operates and the potential for change 'from below'.

For community development, this underlines the need to understand how power works, to challenge dominant discourses and taken-for-granted assumptions, and to make power visible and open to debate. It means that there are opportunities for communities to develop their own narratives of change rather than allowing themselves to become complicit in those dictated by others, and to use the new governance spaces that have emerged both to shape and influence the exercise of government and to promote alternative agendas (Taylor, 2007a).

Levels and dimensions of power

Empowerment has long been part of the language of community practice and community policy, but it is a difficult and somewhat paradoxical concept. It can imply that power is being bestowed on communities and is in someone else's gift (and by implication can be taken away again). The previous sections have discussed some different theories about *who has power* and *how power works*. Sherry Arnstein's (1969) famous ladder of participation addresses the question of *how much power* communities have. She suggests a spectrum of levels of power from non-participation (manipulation and therapy), through degrees of tokenism (informing, consulting and placating) to degrees of citizen power (partnership, delegated power and citizen control). She argues though, that many 'participation' exercises amount to little more than tokenism.

This ladder has been used many times to test out whether participation and 'em'powerment initiatives are giving communities real power over their services, economies and surroundings. It has also been adapted and reworked but also criticised – for assuming that full community control is always the peak of achievement and that communities are homogeneous. In addition, power is dynamic and shifts, and this is a static model. If Arnstein's ladder is to meet these criticisms, it needs to be reapplied over time and used to test how far those who are in control in the community are themselves sharing their power more widely (see for example, Burns et al, 2004).

A more complex model to assess the way in which power is working in communities has been developed by the Institute for Development Studies. Their power cube (www.powercube.net) combines different dimensions of power:

- The first is the form it takes, and this reflects some of the theories about how power works by differentiating between: visible (observable decision making mechanisms; hidden (shaping or influencing the policy agenda); and invisible (shaping norms and beliefs).
- The second relates to the levels at which it operates: household, local, national and global.
- The third differentiates between the different arenas in which power is acted out: closed spaces, where decisions are made by closed groups; invited spaces where communities may be invited to join with external actors but on their terms; and popular or claimed spaces, those that groups form for themselves, determining their own agendas and ways of operating.

They also extend the 'power over'/'power to' distinction to include: power with (collective power, through organisation, solidarity and joint action); and power within (personal self-confidence, often linked to culture, religion or other aspects of identity, a form of power that influences the thoughts and actions that are seen to be legitimate).

The theories discussed here and the power frameworks with which the section finishes can help community development to understand power, how it operates and where the potential might exist to exercise agency and establish new 'circuits of power' (Clegg, 1989). They also address a central question for community development – the question of 'structure' versus 'agency'. How far is the fate of disadvantaged communities determined by external factors? And how far can communities challenge dominant forms of power? The next section explores this question from an institutional perspective, asking how institutions frame the way that groups and organisations operate, or whether complexity theory offers a better understanding in the twenty-first century.

Organisations and institutions: how agency is organised

Many of the scholars we have mentioned are critical of the behaviourist explanations of human behaviour that we mentioned earlier. Such theories suggest that people's behaviour is the result of rational choices they make as self-interested individuals seeking to maximise their benefits and minimise their costs. They do not look behind observable behaviour to consider issues of power, identity, or social or human psychology. Research on communities in partnership suggests that it is also important to understand the institutional pressures on communities when they enter into partnerships with the state or other external actors. For new institutionalists, organisational behaviour is structured by the fields in which people operate and the 'rules of the game' in those fields. These rules may be determined by a variety of forces – competition, the state or professions – and they structure the way organisations behave in three ways (DiMaggio and Powell, 1983):

■ Coercive pressures are imposed by resource providers or cultural expectations.

- Mimetic pressures lead organisations to copy other organisations that are seen to be successful, adopting 'best practice'.
- Normative pressures come from following professional or group norms and values.

These pressures are particularly strong in times of uncertainty – the rise of managerialism may be seen as a particularly powerful example, with managerial conditions sometimes imposed, sometimes copied in the hope that this will provide competitive advantage, or simply accepted as the norm – 'the way we do things now'. However, while communities need to recognise these pressures, they do not have to succumb to them. As Powell later acknowledged, there is scope for compromise or bargaining around government requirements and there are multiple sources of authority and guidance. Organisations may combine influences from dissimilar sources and pressures may be partial, inconsistent or short-lived. Community development can therefore help communities to question the 'rules of the game' by challenging taken-for-granted assumptions about the way meetings are held, for example, encouraging groups to bring their own knowledge and experience to bear or finding alternative role models to follow.

Systems and ecological approaches

The rational choice theories that have been dominant in policy tend to focus on individual self-interest and assume linear models of change, treating individual actors as if they operate in a vacuum. But a number of the theories discussed so far argue the need for a holistic rather than reductionist approach, understanding the behaviour of individuals, groups and organisations as part of a dynamic field or 'system' with independent and interacting parts. They also highlight the complicated dynamics of modern society. Systems models of thinking consider the whole set of organisations or stakeholders operating in a given situation, and the way in which interactions between them influence each other's behaviour (Burns, 2007).

Complexity theory, for example, drawing on a variety of scientific fields, offers a much richer understanding of human behaviour than the rational choice theories of the economist. Complexity models emphasise the interconnectedness of life, suggesting that small-scale local interactions can result in major, unpredictable events (Capra, 1996). They tend to see social progress in terms of the evolution of new solutions or emergent forms of collective organisation, in ways that contrast with more linear explanations of change. They aim to explain two phenomena characteristic of communities operating as complex living systems: the emergence of familiar patterns and the occurrence of unplanned events (Gilchrist, 2009, Chapter Seven). Chaos theory represents an application of complexity thinking, with its most famous example known as the 'butterfly effect', where the flap of a delicate wing is said to precipitate a hurricane on the other side of the world. The implications of complexity theory for community development are that it is important to be prepared for the unexpected and to maximise community connections to provide optimal levels of interaction. Helping people to develop networks and to allow new groupings to emerge from these relationships creates an environment that can enable change and sustain community activity.

Social movement theory

We described earlier the distinction that the power cube makes between closed, invited and 'popular' or 'claimed' spaces. Social movements are perhaps the clearest manifestation of the claimed spaces that the power cube identifies – natural experiments in power, legitimation and democracy (Crossley, 2002, p 9). Social movement theory has borrowed from a range of disciplines to explore the political opportunities for change, the ways in which resources are mobilised for change and the ways in which issues are framed. All three elements have obvious relevance for community development.

Its focus on political opportunity structures shows how changes in the external world determine opportunities for change. Sidney Tarrow (2004) has argued that changes in elites and/or in government may temporarily reduce the capacity for state control and open up possibilities for change in a number of ways. They prompt shifts in political alignments, with conflicts between elites, new access to decision makers and the potential for new allies. They may introduce new institutional provisions for participation. Political openings are not, however, enough. The potential to exploit them will vary according to cultural and sociopolitical factors and opportunities may close again. So it is important to look at the second element of social movement theory referred to earlier: the factors that make for the successful mobilisation and organisation of resources.

At one end of the scale, social movement scholars have stressed the importance of networks in connecting people's personal understanding of their situation to collective action, as a way of making sense of their situation and sustaining a collective identity (Melucci, 1996; Gilchrist, 2009). They highlight the importance of embedding a movement in existing networks, but also refer to the role of boundary spanning connections in spreading its base beyond a narrow homogeneous core. At the other end of the scale, social movement scholars have also begun to pay more attention to the function of social movement organisations (SMOs) as incubators of talent, collectors and disseminators of information and springboards for mobilisation (Caniglia and Carmin, 2005).

SMOs and networks can help to keep movements alive during periods of repression or through ebbs and flows of interest. They allow people to stay in touch with one another, to learn about new developments and to mobilise should the need arise. But opportunity and mobilisation are not enough on their own to account for collective action. A third element of social movement theory concerns itself with the importance of framing – the meanings and definitions that people bring to their situation (McAdam et al, 1996, p 5). As our earlier discussion of discourse and language implied, power can flow as much through meanings as resources. To cite Tarrow, placing a new issue on the agenda in an expressive and challenging way can leave behind permanent expansions in participation, popular culture and ideology (1994, p 188).

Much has been written about the way in which traditional mass movements have given way to a new wave of social movements, organised around identity rather than class and looking for social and cultural transformation rather than political change (Melucci, 1988; Appiah, 2007).The potential of the internet has, it could be argued, further transformed the potential and organisation of social movements. Nonetheless, social movement theory highlights the importance in community development of identifying and capitalising upon opportunities for change, of framing issues in ways that capture the attention of both communities and policy makers and of finding the right balance between formal and informal ways of organising for change.

Brief conclusion

In Chapter Two, we introduced the idea of praxis, demonstrated through action based on informed and considered thinking. If social change is to be achieved, theory and practice need to be in dialogue. But theories develop in different schools and disciplines and only too rarely do they talk to, or inform each other. In this chapter we have introduced some of the theories that help us to think about how communities work, how they interact with the state and their wider environment, how power works and how change might be achieved. In the following chapter, we will be looking at the way community development puts its values and ideas into practice.

Summary

- Theories of community generally differentiate between the organic communities associated with the past and the more functional identity-based communities associated with industrial and post-industrial society.
- Social capital theory suggests that social ties are as important to the health of society and democracy as other forms of capital. But

bridging and linking social capital are as important as bonding social capital if social change is to be achieved.

▪ Theories of self- and collective efficacy emphasise the importance of social context and collective experience. The structural factors that affect communities often undermine efficacy, but community workers can play a role in generating more positive experiences.

▪ Theories of the state can be differentiated between those that see state and community in opposition, and pluralist models in which the state mediates between different interests. The former suggest a radical model of community development; the latter a role as broker helping groups to negotiate the system.

▪ Theories of power can be based on a zero- or positive-sum model. The former tends to emphasise structure, but the latter suggests the potential for agency. The power cube developed by the Institute for Development Studies (www.powercube.net) can help groups to explore different dimensions of power.

▪ Institutional theory explains the pressures on groups and communities to conform, but in a complex society, the interactions between different stakeholders can lead to new forms of organising.

▪ Community development can look to social movement theory to suggest how to identify and maximise opportunities for social change.

Further reading

A short guide can only give readers a brief introduction to the different theoretical approaches that can inform community development and readers are strongly advised to explore the wider literature on the ideas that particularly interest them. There is a growing body of literature on social capital, for example, including books by John Field (2003) and David Halpern (2005), which offer a critical appraisal of its implications for policy. On the web, the reviews of community and social capital in infed (the encyclopaedia of informal reading – www. infed.org) are well worth reading.

The present authors have also explored these ideas further. Alison Gilchrist's *The well-connected community* (2009) shows how ideas of networking and social capital can be used by the community worker, as does Marilyn Taylor's chapter (2007b) in *The handbook of community movements and local organizations*, edited by Ram Cnaan, Carl Milofsky and Al Hunter. Al Hunter's chapter in the same book is a stimulating introduction to concepts of community.

Stephen Luke's *Power: A radical view* (2005) is an excellent and accessible guide to different theories of power and is now in a second edition. The power cube, along with a much fuller discussion of its evolution and ideas, can be found on the web: www.powercube.net. Those who are prepared to engage with more academic prose will find a thorough discussion of governmentality in Peter Miller and Nikolas Rose's book *Governing the present* (2009), particularly the chapter 'The death of the social', and the section within it called 'The birth of the community'. All these texts cover the work of Foucault, but readers can also find an introduction to Foucault's own writing in Rabinow's *The Foucault reader* (1984). Peter Somerville's new book (2011) explores the application of a range of relevant theory to community and community development, while Margaret Ledwith provides an excellent introduction to Gramsci and Freire (1997, 2005). Though published in the 1990s, Sidney Tarrow's classic study of social movements still provides a brilliant overview, as well as ideas on repertoire that community development workers can apply in practice. Much of the theory on power introduced in this chapter is also discussed in more detail in Marilyn Taylor's *Public policy in the community* (2011).

5

effective and ethical community development: what's needed?

This chapter reminds us that important values and principles underpin community development. It considers what is needed to support community development, including the skills and techniques that characterise effective practice. In doing so, it will address debates over whether community development is best seen as a set of skills, an occupation, a set of values, a profession, an intervention or a movement. Much of this chapter focuses on community development work, rather than community development as an approach. It explores the nature of interventions carried out by people who are usually employed to work with communities and who are therefore accountable for their practice. Some of the associated dilemmas and challenges are considered in greater depth in Chapter Seven.

A broad value base

As we have already noted, not everyone who works with communities can be described as a community development worker. However, there are several forms of community practice that contribute to community development, using similar skills and resources (Banks et al, 2003; Butcher et al, 2007). This chapter will examine the skills and strategies generally associated with effective and ethical community development interventions.

Community development is best considered as an approach to working with communities that is informed by an enduring set of principles, as indicated in Chapter Two. These are:

- social justice
- equality
- participation
- empowerment
- collective action
- cooperation
- learning.

Community development has many components. First among these are the unpaid efforts and expertise of members of the community – so-called 'ordinary' residents who take on roles as leaders, volunteers, committee members and so on to set up and run a whole variety of community-based organisations. Working alongside them, especially in the most deprived areas, might be professionally qualified community development workers, who have demonstrated their competence and understanding, often at graduate level. These could be employed by the local authority, a voluntary body, a partnership or occasionally even the community itself, perhaps under the auspices of a tenant-owned housing co-op or residents' association. A recent survey of community development workers found that approximately half were employed in the voluntary sector, with slightly under that proportion based with statutory bodies, mainly local councils but also some health care trusts (Sender et al, 2010).

People in other roles and disciplines also perform aspects of community development even though they do not have the words in their job titles. These may be front-line staff delivering public services such as, for example, police officers, street cleaners, park keepers, housing officials, health visitors or school caretakers. The way they do these jobs can encourage people to share in the responsibility for their environment, raising issues of concern and working in partnership to create solutions that work for local people. If they are approachable, listen well and can use their initiative to take forward the ideas, then they could be said to be part of a broad, usually uncoordinated team that is working to empower communities and develop better relations between the state and the public. In recognition of the value of working in partnership with communities and the voluntary sector, many local councils and the larger housing associations employ community engagement or tenant participation officers who have lead responsibility for implementing strategies to improve dialogue and cooperation between statutory agencies and residents. Backroom staff, such as planners, service managers and communications units can all play their role in making sure that information is available to the public in friendly and timely ways, and that the views of communities are taken on board wherever feasible. This chapter will look at the skills, methods and attitudes that can be deployed generally by institutions to develop communities' sense of their own rights and responsibilities, and their capacity to achieve change.

Although community development is clearly 'people-oriented' and requires skills in working with individuals, groups and organisations, other factors can also contribute to the building of community strengths and capabilities, for example leadership training, but also most notably financial and physical resources that communities can use to help them meet, organise and run activities. Access to, or better still, ownership of some kind of communal building can make a huge difference. This could be as basic as a community room in a block of flats, right through to a purpose-built centre with offices, performance space, sports facilities, a cafe and training rooms. Current policy on the transfer of assets from local authorities to community ownership (see Chapter Three), can make vital resources available for community use, but can also leave communities struggling to maintain them unless they receive some level of community development support. So-called community anchor organisations, such as community associations, councils for voluntary action, settlements or development trusts, add extra value because they act as a generic hub for a range of smaller groups and networks. By providing support, equipment, training and advice, these bodies ensure that communities have access to resources they could not otherwise afford if left to their own devices (Thake, 2001; CLES, 2009). They often act as coordinators of community-led and voluntary initiatives, putting people in touch with relevant organisations and brokering collaborative arrangements across sectors or between different sections of the community, for example, to organise a local festival.

In between, we find a whole variety of premises, including village halls, social clubs, church annexes, redundant shops and former classrooms in schools, which have opened their doors, sometimes after refurbishment, for community use. A community without a meeting place experiences severe difficulties in getting organised and engaging with public bodies on a collective basis.

Box 5.1   A local community-run centre

The INTACT Centre in Preston is an inspiring example of the role of a successful 'anchor organisation' and has developed into its current position as a community-led, professionally run social enterprise over more than two decades. It is firmly embedded in the local area, acting as a hub for many groups and activities, and a 'home from home' for residents who drop in for support and advice, and to meet with others. The Centre has a strong volunteer programme, helping to run a range of clubs and activities, with community members being the majority on the Board of Trustees. The organisation grew out of its first premises and has gradually refurbished and extended a dilapidated prefab building to accommodate a growing team of paid and unpaid workers, including regular placements for social work students.

Over the years the Trust has evolved, by raising its profile in the local community, taking up local issues and encouraging residents to be involved in all aspects of running the Centre. It has received funding from a number of charitable trusts and foundations, to help with staffing and building costs. Recently, a deliberate strategy has developed to work in partnership with public agencies to bid for contracts and investment that will help meet various government objectives. This rebranding and 'market targeting' has enabled the organisation to diversify its income, aim for sustainability and compete successfully for contracts to deliver services on, for example, sexual health,

IT training, children's and young people's activities and employment recruitment.

In addition, the Centre acts as a champion and advocate for the area, drawing in substantial resources and demonstrating that good quality services can be provided in the independent sector, thereby enabling statutory partners to meet their objectives, for example around reduced antisocial behaviour or better health awareness. It is able to use its track record and knowledge of the communities it serves to act as a 'bridge' between the authorities and local people, hosting meetings of the major neighbourhood forum and enabling smaller groups to grow and be better networked. This important community development function has empowered local people by providing forums for dialogue, increasing the strength of local voices, ensuring that people have access to information or signposting them to other agencies which might better serve their needs. Alongside these activities, the Trust works with local residents to organise regular events which bring people together and generate a sense of 'belonging' and community pride. A recent survey of opinion among residents and users showed that INTACT improved well-being, created opportunities, increased community cohesion and generally made a real difference to the quality of life in the area.

Although community development workers may be employed in the voluntary sector, the focus for their work is usually at the level of the community sector: the smaller, less formal groups and networks that have fewer resources and are often run almost exclusively through voluntary effort. Their existence seems to be more precarious and less visible to outsiders and their potential can be overlooked in favour of the more stable and accessible voluntary organisations that may have a local presence but are not always run by local people. It has been conservatively estimated that around two thirds of the independent organisations that make up civil society in the UK could be described as informal or unconstituted community groups (Scott, 2010).

It is sometimes imagined that communities can deliver services for nothing because they mobilise unpaid labour through volunteers and activists, but the probability of success and sustainability is generally enhanced if they have access to professional support, often in the form of community development practitioners. Communities also need money to run their activities, albeit on a smaller scale. They often struggle to raise funds, through jumble sales, raffles, sponsored events or membership. These may cover basic running costs but do not allow for growth and innovation. Even quite small grants for community development can make an enormous difference, such as seedcorn funding for a new initiative, to lease some vital equipment, to arrange an exchange visit or to hire a meeting room. Ideally, these should be readily available and without strings attached, perhaps at the discretion of a local councillor or community development worker. Some areas have experimented with communities having control of a budget that is ring-fenced for community use. These models are known as community chests, local social capital or participatory budgeting. Decisions on the allocation of funds are made at open meetings at which members of the public or community representatives listen to the applicants and agree where the money can best be allocated. These exercises are themselves forms of community development because they are empowering, they build links across communities, raise awareness and encourage a variety of skills, including presentation, advocacy and negotiation. They may, however, need careful preparation and facilitation to make sure that the procedures are transparent and fair.

When getting involved in running community activities, people find they need to develop new skills and knowledge, for example in order to arrange effective and democratic meetings, to take minutes, to organise events or services and so on. They may want or require training in: financial accounting; health, safety and hygiene regulations; protection procedures for children and vulnerable adults; all aspects of computing; staff recruitment and supervision; equalities policy and practice; or any number of topics which are unfamiliar or where existing knowledge needs updating. Adult and community education courses, especially where these are set up in response to community requests, can greatly enhance people's confidence and ability to carry out roles within their community. The learning gained from experience, discussion and observation is also valuable, and as we saw in Chapter Two, community development workers play their part in supporting informal education.

A strategic approach

It has often been said that community development is a long-term process and is most effective when it forms part of a coherent strategy for social improvement across a given area or aims at addressing problems or discrimination experienced by a particular section of society, such as women or older people.

A strategic approach implies some kind of overarching purpose or vision of what will be achieved. It identifies the main features of the current situation and sets out the various steps or objectives that will be undertaken to make progress towards that goal. The strategy would also state who the key stakeholders are and what resources are likely to be required. Community development has suffered in the past from being relatively unstrategic, at a national level and also at district or subregional levels. The *Community development challenge* report, commissioned by the Department for Communities and Local Government and published in 2006, attempted to address this in its analysis of the state of community development at that time and made a series of recommendations regarding the status of the occupation, the evidence base and the need to be more strategic, as well as funding, management and training. These brought together findings from a number of research reports as well as the combined experience of many community practitioners and experts (CLG, 2006).

For community development to become more strategic, there needs to be consideration of at least two aspects simultaneously. Firstly, how can the core of specialist community development workers be better supported and more effective? Secondly, how can community development as a way of working (a set of values and techniques) be better mainstreamed, that is, understood and embedded within general services and organisations that engage with the public on a statutory basis?

Experience of developing community development strategies in local authorities has highlighted a number of benefits and a few obstacles (Community Development Exchange, 2008). The process of discussing and agreeing the strategy can improve relationships among the stakeholders and clarify roles. Making everyone aware of who is undertaking which aspects of community development makes it easier and more probable that these organisations and individuals will be able to cooperate in the future. It creates a foundation for coordinating activities, so that each agency can play its part fairly and effectively in achieving the overall aim of developing the living conditions and capacity of the target communities. Having a shared understanding or definition of community development creates a sense of alignment and mutual support. This recognises that a foundation of community development often contributes towards the policy outcomes of several sectors but raises issues about who owns and takes responsibility for the successful implementation of the strategy.

It is important to acknowledge the drivers for community development and to adjust these according to changing political conditions. For example, during the New Labour government of 1997 to 2010, key policy themes were social inclusion, community empowerment and cohesion. Under the present coalition government, community development must show how supporting active citizens, self-help groups and voluntary associations will help to build the 'Big Society' envisaged by current politicians. The need for efficiency savings during the present recession adds weight to the business case for demonstrating social return on investment, but the evidence for this is somewhat patchy.

Community development does not have a statutory basis in the UK and is therefore vulnerable to cuts as well as seeming peripheral within the broad responsibilities of mainstream public sector organisations. As we shall explore further in Chapter Seven, this is one of the main issues that must be addressed through community development strategies. In particular, a business case is needed to persuade senior officers, funders and politicians that community development offers a cost-effective way of delivering higher level results.

Working with communities

At more local levels, where community development workers are usually deployed, a strategy for developing community capacity, resources and activities must start by getting alongside communities themselves, building relationships with key players and really listening to what people have to say. This is known as a 'bottom-up' approach and contrasts with a more 'top-down' model whereby the agenda is set externally by national targets, area programmes or funders' priorities.

As we saw in Chapter Two, community development is fundamentally concerned with helping communities to help themselves and to achieve greater influence over decisions that affect their lives. Building capacity, overcoming obstacles and acquiring assets are therefore crucial aspects. One of the roles of community development practitioners is therefore to encourage and draw out learning from experience so that community members become individually and collectively more confident and more powerful. Although communities share common characteristics and tend to operate in similar ways, nevertheless the first stage of the work is to really get to know the particular locality or community. This means spending time with a range of people who hold prominent positions in relevant organisations, having conversations about what they do, and listening carefully to discover how they see their issues and opportunities. By helping out, offering supportive advice, observing interactions between community members and asking meaningful questions, the worker is able to form a picture of what's going on as well as enabling people to get to know what he or she has to offer. Once the worker begins to get a sense of the community, its preoccupations, needs, resources and challenges, he or she can work with community members to share suggestions, information or guidance about how certain problems could be addressed, for example by calling a meeting, undertaking some action research, pulling together a campaign group, obtaining funding or getting in touch with organisations which have been in similar circumstances (or all of these). Transformational approaches argue that community development must move from change at community level, scaling up interventions by connecting to social movements and national consortia.

Community development helps people to identify where they have common concerns and aspirations. It supports people to deal with these by working together through collective action and engaging with the relevant authorities. This stage of organisation development may occur at any time and in some instances doesn't happen at all. But if communities find themselves applying for substantial funds, employing staff, managing resources or acting in a representative capacity, then they should probably establish some kind of formally constituted body. These can take many forms and the resultant organisation may or may not choose to seek charitable status. A formal, legally incorporated organisation has the advantage of providing clear mechanisms for decision making, with roles and responsibilities allocated through a constitution and offering some protection for individual members from legal liability. Model formats are available from national organisations, such as the memorandum and articles for community associations, which are needed to establish a company limited by guarantee.

Community development workers should be familiar with the merits and disadvantages of the different organisational forms available to community and voluntary organisations and be able to work with community members to help them decide what model suits their purpose and establish it. And this is only the start. Once they get going, many organisations grow quite rapidly – their profile rises, membership expands, they acquire resources and take on new activities or roles. Structures and procedures may need to be adapted in order to accommodate these changes, particularly if the group needs to become more accountable, more democratic and more inclusive. The advice of an outside professional can be invaluable in this regard as change is often resisted, especially by the 'founders', or those who have more to lose by way of status or control.

Box 5.2   Growing and changing an organisation for older people

Some retired people began to meet regularly to enjoy doing things together such as day trips to local places of interest. A community worker helped them to apply to a charitable trust to cover some of the costs of transport, and suggested that they open up the group to others in the community. They were happy to do this and discovered that many older residents were lonely and needed day-to-day contact to help with household chores and maintenance tasks. The group set up a home visiting service and gradually raised a grant to provide a subsidised 'handyperson'.

In order to safeguard the funds and employ someone in this role, the community worker worked with a small committee to establish the group as a Friendly Society, which later registered for charitable status. As new members came on board, some of the current officers found it difficult to accept the changes needed, but the community worker was able to handle these discussions and allow the original founders to bow out gracefully, while encouraging the others to take on responsibility for running the organisation.

Community development workers are often on hand to help groups and organisations that run into difficulties, perhaps due to an undemocratic or burnt-out leadership, failure to attract new members, personality clashes, ideological disagreements or diverging interests. These problems can reflect internal tensions or changing circumstances. They may require mediation, a rethink of an organisation's priorities or a deeper cultural change to allow new agendas to emerge. Facilitating these discussions, advising on transitions and dealing with the inevitable fall-out are important aspects of the community development role that demand high levels of skill and understanding. On occasion, the best course of action will be to assist an organisation to end, either by merging with another, closing down or going into temporary hibernation. It is also important to consider the wider picture. Community workers need to be aware of the constellation of groups, partnerships and organisations that make up the local community and voluntary sector. Sometimes the most effective course of action may be to forge links with other bodies that can challenge or overcome a particular blockage or come together to seize an opportunity that is too big for a community group to deal with on its own. An important role for practitioners is to maintain an overview of the community's interests, activities and potential so that they can work with people to respond positively to changing circumstances and not necessarily defend the status quo. Encouraging community members to 'let go' of cherished ideas that no longer work and enabling new forms of collaboration to emerge from what has gone before, can be a really valuable contribution to the development of a community, especially if lessons are learnt and shared along the way.

Successful organisations evolve and can be helped to do this through developing wider links, which give access to information about the bigger policy or financial context in which they operate. Community development workers are often to be found setting up and servicing multi-agency networks which bring together people who have overlapping interests but want to retain their autonomy. Being involved in these types of bodies provides community groups with better insights into future threats and opportunities. It allows them to share their ideas with like-minded people and to work collaboratively around common issues. By acting together, communities develop a stronger voice and greater negotiating power with other agencies.

Improving community engagement

Working across organisational and sectoral boundaries has been shown to be a key, but not always recognised feature of community development practice. For workers based in the public sector, for example working for a police authority, their role is crucial in maintaining relations and communication at the interface with communities, particularly the most disaffected or marginalised.

Community development can provide a strong and sustainable foundation for community engagement and citizen empowerment by creating the conditions for more equal dialogue and cooperation and building capacity for it within institutions and communities. On the one hand it enables authorities to understand and work with communities better, changing their somewhat bureaucratic processes and introducing different forms of communication and organising that encourage more diverse participation. Community workers employed by statutory agencies play an important role in challenging taken-for-granted cultures within their own organisations, and can work with colleagues to change structures and procedures that exclude or inhibit community engagement. Within communities, community development creates a wider pool of 'active citizens' who have the confidence, skills and knowledge to act as community leaders or representatives. The network of groups, forums and organisations operating at community level can ensure that these people are supported in their roles and held accountable for their decisions. Thus, community development is a vital ingredient in strategies for increasing the influence and responsibility of communities over the design and delivery of public services, either directly or through involvement in cross-sectoral partnerships.

Box 5.3　Networking to promote health and well-being

The Yorkshire and Humber Empowerment Partnership (YHEP) is part of a national government-funded programme (the National Empowerment Partnership) designed to work at a regional level to promote community empowerment. It does this by working with communities and with public sector partners (particularly local authorities), and by developing networks within and between sectors. For example, the Yorkshire and Humber Community Empowerment in Health and Well-being Network is an emerging network that aims to build the capacity to empower communities to improve their own health and well-being.

It was set up as a result of a health worker participating in and being inspired by a YHEP conference which shared international experience with people across the region. In the spring of 2010, the network had 48 individual members, representing local authorities, primary care trusts, voluntary and community organisations, community activists and freelance consultants. All were involved in health and well-being activities and had an interest in improving partnership working across the region as well as empowering individuals and communities to contribute to planning and decision making about health and well-being activities and services. One of the Network's aims is to share evidence of impact, best practice, information, training and resources, supporting projects to evaluate their activities and outcomes as well as providing a forum for community health champions to have a regional voice.

Source: YHEP (2010)

Core competencies

Over the years, there have been several attempts to define the skills and knowledge required by competent community development workers. The latest of these are the national occupational standards (NOS), developed by the Federation for Community Development Learning following widespread consultation in the field (for a full description see www.fcdl.org.uk/NOS). They are broadly accepted by practitioners, trainers and employers, and are used to write job descriptions and person specifications. Frameworks are also being developed to manage performance, deliver training courses and identify staff development needs.

In order to meet these standards, practitioners are encouraged to reflect on their work, focusing on the *how* and *why* of what they do, as well as specific results. So, for example, it is not sufficient to organise a well-attended public meeting around a local issue; a community development worker would also need to consider how community members have been empowered to influence decisions, and to ensure that no sections of the community have been excluded from participation, that opportunities were created for collaboration and that the agenda was largely set by the community rather than imposed externally.

The skills and techniques for successful community development include being able to work effectively with individuals, groups, networks and organisations. They can be categorised as relating to people, places, information, resources, systems and self.

People and places

Being able to work with people is probably the most significant area of competence for community development. Good community development workers will be active listeners, empathising with what they hear and able to establish rapport with a wide range of people. They will understand the diversity of cultures and abilities among the community they are working with, and be sensitive to differences as well as being aware of inequalities and tensions between different groups. They will be able to encourage people to take on roles or tasks that will stretch them a little, and to challenge prejudices or practices that are oppressive. As we shall explore further in Chapter Seven, this may involve dealing with negative emotions such as fear, resentment, anger and hurt, in addition to tackling damaging and discriminatory attitudes.

Mostly, community development work is about encouraging people to think creatively, devise solutions, work together, address leadership issues and resolve conflicts. This requires skills in persuasion, negotiation and informal coaching, usually on a one-to-one basis but occasionally as part of the support given to a group. It is also important to recognise when to 'let go', to enable the community members to continue on their own journey towards independence, partnership or engagement.

Working with volunteers

While community development workers will not generally be called upon to carry out the maintenance of buildings or equipment themselves, they may find it useful to know what's involved and how these tasks can be managed, either by volunteers or by bringing in contractors. Volunteers are an essential part of the resource base for community groups and being able to support and coordinate their efforts may be an underestimated aspect of the role. The term 'volunteer' is used here to include anyone who has made a free choice to be involved in a community group or activity and is not being paid for their contribution (though they may receive out-of-pocket expenses). A volunteer could therefore be a parent or childminder helping to run the local toddlers group. The committee members of the estate tenants' group are volunteers, as are the community representatives on the crime reduction partnership board. After-school clubs and youth centres may have professional trained workers but are often assisted by a team of dedicated volunteers, all of whom have to be vetted and supervised. Community activists are also volunteers, often putting in long hours in pursuit of their passion or running campaigns. People taking on more formal roles, such as school governor, do so on a voluntary basis, as 'active citizens' playing their part in promoting civic responsibility. Attempts to force people to 'volunteer' are counterproductive to the spirit of free choice, and mandatory schemes such as community service for offenders or people applying for British citizenship should not fall within the remit of community development.

Working with members of the community who are volunteering their time and energy is a normal facet of community development that gives rise to a number of challenges that aren't generally encountered when dealing with paid staff with clear job descriptions and positions in the hierarchy. People who are active in their own communities and in pursuit of their own collective goals do not necessarily see themselves as volunteers in the traditional sense and they may have an uneasy relationship with paid community workers allocated to serve their interests. Some community activists lack confidence. Others can display dogmatic arrogance or single-minded devotion to their 'cause'. It can require great skill and diplomacy to find out how best individual members of the community can most effectively contribute and be rewarded for their efforts. While they are to some extent free agents, there are inevitably expectations (and some regulations) that govern their involvement, especially where the welfare of children or vulnerable adults is concerned. Helping volunteers to make full use of their talents, to surprise themselves, to learn from each other and to work as part of a team is essential to community development. Volunteers come from all walks of life. They may range from high performing mavericks, used to getting their own way, through to dedicated leaders and followers, including individuals with low self-esteem and possible mental health issues. As well as offering much-needed time and skills, they often bring emotional demands and discriminatory attitudes. All this needs careful handling and clarity. Such difficulties can be compounded when the worker is line-managed by a member (often the chair) of a voluntary management committee.

Relationships of trust and mutual respect are vital for community development as they are the foundation for collective action and empowerment. Helping community members to develop 'meaningful interaction' and to work together for common goals requires skills and understanding in how people, often holding widely differing views, can connect and communicate on their shared interests. Community development workers often play a mediating or networking role, helping people and groups to find potential allies and to set up partnership arrangements between different bodies (Gilchrist, 2009). This means acknowledging and tackling some of the frictions and stresses caused by diverse backgrounds or competing expectations, especially when these are exacerbated by social biases and intolerance.

In order to be able to work with people in ways that are both sympathetic and stimulating, community development workers need a good understanding of the locality in which they are based – its history, key players, organisational networks, current pressures and future aspirations. Finding out about the place can be achieved through carrying out a systematic community profile to map the various organisations operating in the area, identify significant geographical features, audit social needs and establish a picture of the demographics or population make-up (Hawtin and Percy-Smith, 2007). It is useful to know something about the history and customs of communities living in the area, as well as their aspirations for the future. Do people from different backgrounds mix or are there antagonisms that tend to keep some community members apart on a day-to-day basis? Other factors to investigate might be patterns of migration, living standards and health. How does the local economy function and how has it changed in recent years? What about transport connections and the reputation of the area to outsiders? What facilities does the locality enjoy? What is lacking? Are there plans for its regeneration or other improvement strategies being developed by the authorities? And perhaps most importantly, how are things changing and what do residents want to see changed?

Managing information and resources

Community development must start from 'where people are at now', not where we think they should be. Accurate information and clear communication are therefore core competences for the worker. Someone working with a community should know how to access relevant information about that community from formal sources such as the media, census figures, surveys or data on levels of deprivation. This may involve being able to interpret and apply the findings from recent research or consultation exercises. Crucially, it requires the worker to be able to glean information from informal observations and encounters, and to understand the meaning within conversations, stories and traditions. Sometimes this can be conveyed non-verbally, though body language, pictures, graffiti or the appearance of buildings. And then there are myriad rumours and gossip that are also vital forms of communication.

Keeping track of all this information can be challenging to say the least, requiring either an excellent memory or more probably good record keeping. Information technology has developed rapidly in recent years, allowing sophisticated databases to be created and interrogated to create up-to-date knowledge of communities and their environments. Web 2.0 software has led to a whole new form of community development, with local neighbourhood websites, blogs and chat forums providing platforms for inter- and intra-community communication. Evidence suggests that these enable people to engage with local decision making and collective initiatives even if they are at first reluctant to come to public meetings or become involved in face-to-face interactions (Burrows et al, 2005). Presentation and media skills are vital for communities to counter myths and negative images. Community workers can work with local people to challenge these and to offer alternative 'stories' that change public awareness and understanding. In Chapter Eight, we flag up future possibilities for the use of new communication technologies and note that current political trends are towards much greater transparency in sharing information between government bodies and communities.

Community development workers are often themselves trusted sources of information and have a responsibility to share what they know (unless there are grounds for confidentiality) and to enable communities to develop their own means of communication. This means understanding the dynamics of local communication systems – the mechanisms and conventions for sharing ideas and knowledge, the way information flows through a community and the mechanisms by which communities can articulate their views to leaders, representatives and decision makers. However, communities rarely speak with one 'voice' and community development workers need to be confident in facilitating discussion, managing dissent and mediating conflicts.

Encouraging dialogue and debate are crucial aspects of the role, and this can take considerable skill, especially when feelings are running high. There are, however, a range of tools and techniques available that can help meetings to reach consensus or to set priorities.

| **Box 5.4** | **A model for empowerment practice** |

Ketso is a toolkit first developed in southern Africa to help communities be involved in planning village improvements. It consists of a portable set of branches and leaves made out of material that can be written on and stuck to panels to aid reflection, discussion and decision making. It encourage creative problem solving and has been successfully used by communities to plan how to develop a sustainable strategy for food production and sales in Swaziland, to explore budget cuts relating to Portsmouth harbour and to set up a social enterprise for a network of creative artists. It is said to boost confidence and hope, while making sure that people share information and ideas with relevant stakeholders.

Source: www.ketso.com

Successful community development work will result in the acquisition of resources that needs to be managed and maintained. Community development workers often play a key role in helping groups to obtain the resources they need to achieve their goals. Usually this is some kind of funding, which might be used to buy staff or equipment, and may result in the acquisition of a building or other facilities, such as an all-weather sports court. The competences associated with resources include all aspects of fundraising: knowledge of potential sources for grants and donations, being able to work with communities to draw up a budget and put together an application for funding, and a rudimentary grasp of financial accounting to make sure that money is properly spent and recorded.

Systems: policies and procedures

Communities are part of large social, economic and political systems and community development workers need to know how to operate within these and also how to change them if necessary. They should have some political acumen, understand the policy making process and realise how to be effective on committees and working groups. Having a good understanding of the wider context and systemic pressures will make them more effective as negotiators and, where necessary, able to oppose the abuse of power or information.

A good community worker will be alert to opportunities to exert influence and obtain resources, perhaps by exploiting uncertainties or divisions between decision makers, or by finding allies in unexpected places. As Chapter Four suggests, there is much to be learnt from the experience of social movement activists, especially in relation to levering open 'cracks' in the system and mobilising people around a common cause. The practice of community development is potentially affected by a plethora of policies and organisational procedures, some of which may be contradictory. Workers, activists and managers need to have up-to-date knowledge of what is currently in place as well as understanding how to change things. For example, a tenant participation officer for a large housing association was able to use the organisation's policies on antisocial behaviour and equalities to ensure that residents experiencing homophobic harassment were protected, while the perpetrators were moved to a different estate with both support and sanctions in place to encourage them to change their attitudes. A thorough knowledge of the relevant procedures meant that the victims' privacy was respected and they gained much-needed security in their own home. The association's commitment to equality for all tenants led to a mini-poster campaign in the area, which in turn generated a great deal of discussion.

Self: training, learning and reflection

Community development emphasises the value of experiential learning, with many people starting their career as community activists and volunteers. Informal learning, through reflection, discussion, observation and practice, provides a strong basis for learning at all levels. For people who are new to community development there are taster sessions or stand-alone workshops offering an introduction to community development or offering a chance to develop skills in group work, fundraising, running meetings or similar techniques. These are complemented by short courses that may be relevant to particular applications for community development, such as health, regeneration, equalities and so on. There are a range of recognised qualifications in community development, many based on the national occupational standards. Community workers are themselves trainers and educators, albeit usually through informal means, and they should have skills in running workshops, supporting action learning, facilitating dialogue and knowing how to question and learn in order to improve their own practice.

Finally, community development workers depend on their personal values, commitment and characteristics. They must understand how to make use of self – their identity as an employee, but also their identities as members of different communities, possibly including their local neighbourhood. Reflexive practice and good supervision will encourage people to explore how different facets of their lives are relevant to their work, and what biases these might entail.

Brief conclusion

Community development takes time, commitment, resources, practical skills and a huge amount of trust. It does not offer a quick fix to society's problems; rather it is an approach to working with communities that builds relationships, acknowledges people's contributions and capabilities, and aims to address shared problems through collective solutions. It requires more than a set of skills, resources and competences, being based on principles, processes and beliefs that ensure that communities are empowered, that individuals are encouraged and that groups are enabled to achieve their own ends to the benefit of others across the wider society.

Summary

■ Community development takes place in many different settings but is shaped by a set of agreed principles.
■ People working in non-community development jobs use Community development skills to improve community engagement and services.
■ Helping communities to acquire and manage funds and assets provides vital resources for further development.
■ Relatively 'light touch' community development support can make a huge difference to the success of community-led initiatives.
■ Community development can be both generalist and specialist.
■ A more strategic approach is needed to secure its occupational base and investment in communities.
■ Community development helps people to make connections and to build collective capacity.
■ There are a recognised set of standards that define the core competencies needed for effective practice.
■ These form the basis for training, recruitment and performance management.

Further reading

The *Community development challenge* report (CLG, 2006) and subsequent books on management, evaluation and democracy are useful snapshots of the main thinking from practitioners. The national occupational standards (NOS) (FCDL, 2009a) have recently been revised and set out the different roles and skills required for effective community development. The summary framework of key work areas and tasks provides an overview of what can be expected.

There are also numerous guides on community engagement in different settings, many available from the Community Development Foundation. In particular *Setting up for success* (Allen and May, 2007) is an excellent practical guide to working with community groups, as is the Skinner and Wilson (2002) guide, *Assessing community strengths*.

6

applying community development in different service areas

Community development can contribute to outcomes in many different policy fields: cohesion and integration, community safety and crime reduction, culture and the arts, education, environment and sustainable development, health and well-being, housing and local economic development among them. Much of the early community development in the 1960s and 1970s focused on housing, leisure and play, for example, since these were the issues raised by residents in the public housing estates where many community workers were based. Community development workers supported campaigns for housing improvement and rehabilitation and helped to form and provide support for residents' associations. They also supported residents in campaigning for play and leisure facilities and running playgroups and community centres.

By building 'bridging social capital', community development also plays an important role in fostering community cohesion. It can help 'new' communities to settle, providing information and advice about local services, for example, or guidance on their entitlements and responsibilities. It can also help them to form their own associations and support groups and to be involved in wider initiatives such as local festivals or forums. Conversely, by providing advice and 'myth-busting' information, and promoting cultural awareness, community development gives 'host' communities a better understanding of the newcomers and helps them to welcome new communities more readily. People who are confident in their collective or cultural identities are more likely to engage with others beyond their community. Community

---

91

development can support both incoming and 'host' communities to develop this confidence.

Box 6.1   **Sowing the seeds of solidarity**

The Comfrey Project in Newcastle runs allotment sessions for refugee and asylum seekers. As well as enabling the members to grow food for eating, attendance has improved their English and increased levels of interaction with other residents and allotment users. There is a shared lunch and members are encouraged to join other community activities in their areas. They are also referred to other agencies if they need specialist advice or support. As a result of socialising in this safe space, confidence has increased and the prejudice against refugees has also been reduced as local people become aware of the situation of the refugee and asylum seekers and hear the true stories of why they had to leave their home countries.

Source: www.comfreyproject.org.uk

Fear of crime and community safety are other issues that concern both policy makers and local communities. Community development has worked with the victims of crime to set up support groups and to organise campaigns that highlight particular kinds of assault and harassment such as those based around hate and prejudice, drug dealing or antisocial behaviour. Community development approaches have also been used by public authorities and voluntary organisations to improve community safety, for example in relation to arson, traffic accidents and domestic violence. These have often involved public and peer education about risks, but there has also been a commitment to listening to community concerns, developing solutions that will work in given circumstances and generally trying to improve relations between community members and public services, such as the police, fire fighters and planners.

Fear of crime is a real issue in many disadvantaged communities. On the one hand, it makes people unwilling to engage; on the other, it can be whipped up in ways that result in vigilante campaigns – against paedophiles and drug dealing for example. By developing informal social networks and strategies to report milder forms of vandalism or dangerous and antisocial behaviour, community development can increase people's sense of local pride and mutual responsibility, break down barriers and give them the confidence to address more serious issues.

Community development can also help to address the educational underachievement that characterises many poorer communities. People there are often resistant to anything that smacks of formal education, since it has failed them in the past. Community development can build links between schools or colleges and their communities, which give communities access to new resources. It can involve parents in their children's education – a particularly important role in neighbourhoods where educational attainment over the generations has been low. It can also provide informal education opportunities for those whose formal educational attainment is low. This may give people the confidence to re-engage with more formal systems, but it also demonstrates the value of alternative approaches to education, which release and value people's own knowledge, and build the skills and confidence to engage as citizens on their own terms.

| Box 6.2 | Community learning and education for change |

The workers' education movement has a long history in different parts of the global North from the Workers' Educational Association in the UK, to the Danish Folk High Schools and spreading post colonialism to many parts of the globe. It has continued to underpin community development approaches to emancipatory education. Another influence has been the development of leadership programmes for social change in the communities that suffered most from the injustices of society, through organisations like the Highlander Institute in Tennessee and the Industrial Areas Foundation in Chicago (founded in 1932 and 1940 respectively). Both traditions emphasise learning through action to promote change. This approach also lives on through a number of international capacity building agencies (such as Civic Driven Change in the Netherlands, and the Society for Participatory Research in Asia, based in India), trade union initiatives and work with tenants of social housing (for example, the National Tenants Resource Centre in England).

In these and other policy areas, therefore, community development workers support communities in campaigning for better services, in negotiating with service providers and in running their own services. They help communities to access the information and other resources they need and help to demystify professional interventions. They work with professionals, too, to help them understand and respond to community needs.

In the rest of this section, we focus more closely on the contribution community development can make in four particular policy fields. The first three are very much at the forefront of current policy: environmental action, economic development and poverty reduction. The fourth is the arts, and demonstrates the contribution that arts and cultural activities can make to community development and community cohesion. In each case, we set the policy context, ask what community development can offer and highlight some of the challenges that the policy field poses for community development.

Environmental protection and sustainable development

Context

Over the past few decades, there has been a growing realisation that climate change matters and that humans have a responsibility to share the environment more responsibly, both with one another but also with other species that occupy the planet. We know that earth's resources are limited and are not being used fairly. The principle of environmental justice is sometimes included among community development values and refers to people's right to live in a decent, clean and healthy environment with a fair share of the earth's resources and an acknowledgement that future generations should have a similar expectation. The organisation Capacity Global explains it as being based on notions of social justice and equality, with an added slant towards green issues (see www.capacity.org.uk). There is more awareness of the impact of global warming and the need to reduce what has become known as our 'carbon footprint'. There are many claims to the origin of the slogan, 'Think globally, act locally', including the community organiser, Saul Alinksy. But whoever first coined the phrase, it is clear that communities, government and individuals need to take action to safeguard the environment and ensure that future growth is sustainable.

Recent government programmes, such as Every Action Counts, have encouraged voluntary and community organisations to change their ways under five headings: save energy, travel wisely, save resources, shop ethically and care for the local environment (see www.justact. org.uk). Communities have responded with a whole range of initiatives, including food production, community-based renewable energy generation, nature conservation, recycling and awareness raising (Walker et al, 2007). Some of these have been developed through social enterprises, others have attempted to adopt a whole system approach, such as in the 'transition towns', while most have been more piecemeal, with different groups devising actions that suit their circumstances and resources.

In some cases, communities have worked with local authorities to develop larger scale schemes around transport and housing, for example to build sustainable apartment blocks or create safe routes to schools to encourage children to walk or cycle rather than be dropped off in cars by their parents. These have been designed to make it easier for people to protect the environment within their everyday lives.

Box 6.3	Generating energy and income for community benefit

In the US, a not-for-profit company, *Native*Energy supports innovative renewable energy projects in collaboration with Native American tribes, family farmers and other socio-economically disadvantaged communities. These projects include wind farms and methane digesters, which reduce the demand for energy from non-renewable sources. In addition to reducing carbon emissions, the entrepreneurs have adopted a model of community involvement that increases social equity and invests for the future. The 'environmental benefits', that is, carbon offsets, are sold to consumers in the form of notional 'green tags' whose value accrues over the lifespan of the project, estimated at 15 to 25 years. This allows for long-term planning and investment in new technologies.

Source: www.nativeenergy.com

What can community development offer?

There are many ways in which community development supports environmental action and a number of 'clean and green' initiatives have been promoted by government and local authorities. These include neighbourhood agreements drawn up by partnerships of residents and councils, setting out responsibilities concerning street cleaning, abandoned cars, the state of local parks in relation to dog mess and litter, and so on. Community 'clean-ups' and 'litter picks' can be organised at very local levels, for example by the parish council, or they can form part of national campaigns to 'keep Britain tidy'.

Increasingly, communities are reclaiming abandoned sites for public use, creating community gardens or space for growing food. 'Guerrilla gardening', as it has become known recently, received official encouragement from the Prime Minister himself, and under the 'Big Society' rhetoric, there are moves to set up 'friends of' groups to manage local parks, replacing council maintenance teams. Communities are themselves often concerned about threats to their local area from pollution, building developments (on green space) or the arrival of a superstore displacing shops that sell locally produced food and wares. Community development helps them to organise around these issues, mobilising protestors and ensuring that counter-arguments are well presented and persuasive.

Community development can also put people in touch with what's happening elsewhere, for example arranging visits to places where a community-owned energy source has been established, such as a wind turbine that generates electricity for the residents with any surplus being sold to the national grid and the profits being used for community benefit. Recycling schemes can be especially effective, both creating income from waste management contracts and also enabling people to swop, share and trade the resources that are surplus to their personal requirements. This reduces levels of consumption of new goods, tackling poverty as well as reducing demand on landfill sites (Seyfang, 2009). It also creates a sense of community as people make connections through neighbours or websites such as Freecycle or Toolshare.

As Rowan et al (2009, p 10) explain:

> Resource recovery goes beyond recovering value, in pounds or tonnes, from beds, bikes and planks of wood. It includes enabling individuals to recover their own resourcefulness, valuing themselves and others, through second-chance training opportunities or volunteering skills to their community. Resource recovery is about relationships and networks

linking people together to make a practical difference, especially where individuals and communities are under pressure. It is as much about the human recovery as it is about material resources.

Using informal education, community development also encourages greater awareness of climate change and empowers people to organise events which bring together local, regional and national bodies concerned with different aspects of environmental protection.

Box 6.4   Galvanising community action on the environment

A Southampton church ran a successful 'green fair' attended by over 400 people, keen to associate themselves with 'eco-actions'. The planning group reached out beyond the congregation to involve interested individuals as well as organisations such as cycling campaigns, Friends of the Earth and the local sustainability forum. This broad-based approach, tapping into a variety of networks, meant that publicity went out beyond the 'usual suspects' and drew in people from local communities who might not otherwise have turned up to an event about the environment.

There were the usual stalls and activities, but also a political session with the MP and a presentation from the university oceanographic department on the impact of climate change on sea life. Posters displayed ideas that people could use to decide what they could do for themselves, such as composting more waste or joining a car club, and the evaluation form included a page where people could indicate what actions they would be taking as a result of attending the event.

Challenges

For disempowered people living in degraded streets or barren rural areas, it can be difficult to accept some responsibility for a global threat. Communities will only be motivated to protect their environment if they feel that they have some stake in it at a local or personal level. The challenge is to find an issue that people not only feel they have in common, but also one where they believe that their actions can make a difference.

For many people experiencing poverty and discrimination, the environment might not seem a major priority, even though pollution, traffic, diminishing resources and rising costs of energy hit the poor hardest, and they usually have fewer means of escape or protection. We have witnessed how environmental disasters such as hurricanes, floods, mudslides and forest fires have wiped out homes and livelihoods for subsistence populations in developing countries. Environmental justice applies equally to communities the world over.

Local economic development

Context

One of the many problems facing disadvantaged communities is the lack of jobs and businesses, and consequent low levels of money circulating in the local economy. As we shall see in the next section, regeneration programmes have used community development with varying degrees of success. Here we focus on community-generated initiatives using social marketing approaches that bring together needs with offers and resources (skills, energy, motivation) available in the community. Social and community enterprises generally have social benefits for those involved as well as aiming to be financially self-sufficient, with profit reinvested in developing the business. They usually have a strong ethical basis and aim to meet needs that are not being addressed through the commercial market or statutory sector.

There are several ways in which communities can address common financial needs and contribute to growing the local economy. They can develop people-led initiatives that meet real needs, building on local traditions of self-help, communal ownership and mutual exchange. Communities often already have the culture and infrastructure for volunteer involvement and forming coalitions with similar businesses or schemes. Above all, community-based economic development will ensure that there is maximum recirculation of money within the community and that profits are reinvested for mutual benefit.

Financial exclusion is endemic in many communities and is likely to get worse following the recent banking crisis. Not everyone can take for granted services such as financial advice, low interest loans, bank accounts or mortgages. When money is short, people often fall into debt on a temporary but regular basis. A cheap and accessible borrowing scheme can help them to avoid the doorstep lenders, commonly known as loan sharks, and credit unions have developed in many communities to provide savings and loans facilities that members run themselves, often from shop-front premises or a room in a community building. The Grameen bank is an internationally known version of micro-loan arrangements whereby small groups of savers and borrowers, for example the women of a village or a fishing cooperative, are able to pool their money in order to lend to members when they need it or when they have an idea for setting themselves up in business (such as buying a sewing machine or a piece of agricultural equipment). Such schemes are based on relationships of mutual trust and experience very few problems of people defaulting on the loans. Cooperatives and friendly societies, as their names suggest, similarly offer ways in which communities can act collectively to run joint ventures.

Increasingly, statutory services are seeking to work in partnership with voluntary and community organisations to deliver services and co-produce broad outcomes through preventative work. These may be through contracts for specific outputs (such as providing support to families at risk of having children taken into care) or they may involve partnership arrangements with one party providing one kind of resources (for example funding) and communities supplying the rest (voluntary work, local expertise, publicity and so on). With encouragement from central government in relation to policies to promote community empowerment, local authorities are supporting communities to find ways of generating income by transferring assets, such as housing stock, redundant buildings, facilities or land, so that local people can adapt these for their own activities while also taking on responsibility for managing them for communal use. Sometimes these assets are transferred for a nominal 'peppercorn' sum. In other cases, communities raise the purchase price through issuing community bonds or shares. Possible areas for economic involvement by communities have been identified as food and catering, accommodation, care services, small-scale technical projects, energy, water supply, waste recycling, repairs, transport, cultural and heritage activities, environmental protection, leisure and recreation.

What can community development offer?

Community development can help by creating the conditions and capacity for communities to run their own services and produce goods that people are willing to buy. This might involve encouraging local individuals to develop an idea, identify potential markets, suggest likely investors and contact customers. Community development can work to develop people's capacity by increasing skills and knowledge required to run a business, building confidence and developing an array of relationships that will support individuals, organisations and groups. Communities may well need access to external resources, such as technical expertise, financial advice or information about competitors to help them assess and manage the risks involved in running a business, including taking on paid staff. Community development finance institutions are possible sources of affordable loans and advice for start-ups in deprived communities, and have the backing of government (see www.cdfa.org.uk).

Box 6.5   Asset-based social enterprise

In Spalding, Lincolnshire, a disused Victorian railway station has been taken over and turned into a complex of facilities for community use. South Holland Radio is a community interest company that invests any surplus it generates from broadcasting back into the community. In addition to the radio studio where young people try their hand at producing programmes, the organisation runs an outreach scheme to provide a handyman for those who need help with odd jobs in the home, and also supports migrants to learn English. There are plans to set up a community cafe and to rent out spare rooms to other community groups as a way of raising income.

Source: www.shradio.co.uk

As with other applications of community development, strategies for economic and financial inclusion follow certain principles. They involve a process of building from the bottom up, tackling biases and obstacles in order to be as inclusive as possible, encouraging experiential learning and accreditation, dealing with staff and customers on the basis of fairness and transparency and empowering community members to contribute to decision making about the direction of work.

Challenges

Community-based economic development should lead to holistic and sustainable regeneration. It aims to improve access for marginalised communities to training, work opportunities, equipment and loans. But it is difficult to generate investment or income among already poor communities. Recent research by IPPR (Cox and Schmueker, 2010) indicates that many enterprises continue to rely on grants several years into their existence, and there is a high failure rate. Community share schemes depend on people buying into ownership, often with substantial amounts that less affluent households simply do not have spare. There is a risk therefore that community and mutual ownership arrangements reinforce economic and power inequalities, unless community development work is undertaken to inculcate a sense of shared access and belonging for all beneficiaries. A values-based framework highlighting independence, autonomy, self-control and democracy could go some way towards guaranteeing that community-based approaches to economic development do not get subsumed in larger scale programmes (Woodin et al, 2010).

Some of the obstacles relate to the current recession, with access to credit drying up and potential entrepreneurs falling out with one another as pressures build. Cuts in local authority funding are likely to make them more risk adverse in terms of contracts for services, with commissioning processes favouring larger private and voluntary sector organisations. Communities may need to form consortia in order to win and manage contracts and to compete within supply chains. There are considerable risks involved in this approach, especially for relatively small and inexperienced community groups. By joining forces, these can be mitigated to some extent, but collaboration is often complicated, with its own set of risks that need to be anticipated and carefully handled. Furthermore, despite the rhetoric about citizens running services, the current legal and policy framework is ambivalent towards community ownership. Continuing confusion will make people and authorities more reluctant to experiment with a return to tried, but not yet trusted solutions.

Regeneration and poverty reduction

Regeneration in the community

Tackling spatial concentrations of disadvantage has been a feature of urban policy for decades – at least since the US War on Poverty declared by Lyndon Johnson in the 1960s. As indicated in Chapter Three, that era saw a range of initiatives put in place in the US and elsewhere that invested in a comprehensive, research-based approach –

working with communities and local services – to solving the problems of urban deprivation.

During the 1980s, government regeneration initiatives gave priority to economic and physical redevelopment approaches to regeneration. More recent policy initiatives have, however, returned to a more holistic approach and, at least in principle, embraced the need to engage communities if regeneration is to be sustainable.

Box 6.6   A comprehensive approach to regeneration

The 2001 National Strategy for Neighbourhood Renewal in England and parallel initiatives in the other UK countries emphasised the need to put communities 'at the heart of' neighbourhood renewal and to bring community knowledge to bear in developing strategies for renewal. Their holistic approaches aimed to tackle issues of worklessness, community safety, educational underachievement and poor health, and to improve housing and the environment in the most disadvantaged areas. Their strategy was to make services more responsive, to improve local economies and to improve governance, as well as building the social capital that could itself improve the quality of life in fragmented neighbourhoods.

Service providers have been encouraged to 'join up', working in more coordinated ways that make sense to the communities they serve. Communities have also been encouraged, along with the wider third sector, to take on service delivery roles. Parallel strategies have been adopted in other EU countries, for example the *Grands Contrats de Ville* in France, *Kvarterluft* in Denmark and Big Cities Policy/Our Neighbourhoods Turn in the Netherlands. On the wider world stage, the World Bank has promoted Community Driven Development as an integral part of its poverty reduction strategy.

Over the years, these policy initiatives have been matched, sometimes prompted, by action from communities themselves. Communities have banded together to oppose redevelopment, to protest the loss of jobs and to campaign for better services and conditions. Previous sections describe some of the actions they have taken to address the economic and environmental challenges they face. Sometimes supported by government funding, sometimes not, communities have developed their own community-based enterprises, like the community development corporations already mentioned in the US and many community development trusts in the UK. These may be a response to threats of redevelopment, to the closure of local industry or to the failure of public services, or they may be the continuation of a government-funded initiative once the funding comes to an end. Communities have also taken myriad initiatives to improve the quality of life in their neighbourhoods without external prompting – from developing play provision to clean-up campaigns to fighting crime.

What can community development offer?

Investment in community development has been a central feature of many regeneration and poverty reduction initiatives across the globe. Insofar as they recognise and address the multiple causes of poverty and disadvantage at a neighbourhood or settlement level, such initiatives would seem to provide a natural home for the holistic community development approach and its social justice values.

A recent UK review of the evidence on community participation (Pratchett et al, 2009) suggests that the most successful initiatives have access to specialist support. Community development has supported people to express their concerns, campaign for change and take action themselves to address common problems. It has also been essential as a precursor to major government initiatives, raising awareness on both sides, and supporting communities to have an informed voice in planned initiatives and sometimes to oppose external proposals and develop their own plans. It has provided the expertise for communities to develop their own enterprises and bring jobs and wealth into the community. It supports community engagement in partnerships, helping to provide the resources and back-up that other partners take for granted. Crucially, community development support ensures that engagement goes beyond the most committed few, building and spreading leadership skills and ensuring that community leaders are accountable to their wider constituencies.

Challenges

Community development is only one part of the solution to the complex issues facing the most disadvantaged communities. It cannot tackle the structural and economic factors that concentrate the poorest and most vulnerable citizens in social housing and that, some would argue, are inherent in capitalism. Evaluations of many of the initiatives referred to earlier find that achievements – while they may be significant to those involved – are limited and short lived. Critics argue that initiatives to encourage community self-help and community managed services are a mere sticking plaster and risk making those who are the casualties of change responsible for managing their own exclusion. For community development, this poses difficult choices between supporting such initiatives at community level and helping communities to challenge policies that continue to reinforce their exclusion.

This also highlights the need to work beyond the neighbourhood, getting community voices heard at higher levels of government and linking marginalised communities with wider social movements. This helps also to overcome the shortcomings of targeted initiatives that, while they allow for more in-depth work, leave many disadvantaged people outside their boundaries. In addition, the political will for such initiatives is difficult to sustain – there are few votes in it.

Evaluations have highlighted the need to change public service cultures and to mainstream change – an imperative that extends across all policy fields. In many disadvantaged areas, there is considerable mistrust between residents and municipal governments, while the flight from public service investment leaves those that remain demoralised and undervalued. In many localities, too, community engagement translates into information giving or consultation – a very low point on Arnstein's ladder (1969). Where powers are shared with communities, this sharing is often accompanied by levels of monitoring and risk management that stifle creativity and discourage innovation. Community development therefore needs to work by identifying and strengthening allies, spotting and widening opportunities within the system and building relationships across the barriers.

Finally, community responses are not always constructive or inclusive. At worst, the stresses and racial tensions in marginalised neighbourhoods have erupted in rioting and gang warfare. To an extent, exclusion breeds exclusion and the lack of choice faced by residents exacerbates tensions between residents and neighbours that are hard to resolve. This requires considerable skill in mediation and conflict resolution, as well as safe spaces in which tensions can be addressed and the real causes of exclusion explored.

Community arts and culture

Arts in the community

The terms 'art' and 'culture' are often associated with wealth, power and the elite. But between them, art and culture offer a route through which many people engage in local community and public life. Robert Putnam (1993) recognised this when he gave choirs as one example of the activities that produce social capital. For many under authoritarian rule, art and cultural activities have been the only means of expressing and maintaining solidarity, as the folk societies in Hungary and elsewhere in Central and Eastern Europe demonstrated during the Soviet era. State suppression of such activities only serves to demonstrate their power. Art also provides more overt symbols of resistance – it is the songs and images of a campaign or social movement that live on in people's minds.

Arts and culture can also be a potent instrument of social change. Their immediate appeal reaches people that other kinds of intervention cannot reach. They can involve people in many different ways. Art also crosses boundaries. Globalisation has brought the people's art into homes across the world, whether it be music, graffiti or the artefacts of indigenous cultures.

The benefits of arts and cultural activities may be individual: research suggests that they build confidence and self-esteem as well as giving people opportunities to learn new skills. They give people a voice and are powerful tools for learning. The benefits are also collective – these activities can forge a community identity and generate community pride. They provide opportunities for people to socialise and work together. They also allow marginalised communities to be seen and heard in the outside world, changing the image of an area and bringing outsiders in. By providing safe spaces for expression, they can increase understanding and bridge ethnic and generational divides. Conversely, street murals and marches can be used to stake out territory in sectarian fashion, such as has been the case in Northern Ireland.

Box 6.7	**Linking the generations**

Magic Me has been working in East London since 1989 to bridge intergenerational divides. Its projects have used storytelling, creative writing, photography, weaving, drama, dancing, puppetry, carnival, mosaic, ceramics, painting and poetry to bring together young and old participants. They are based in careful preparation, exploring stereotypes, addressing fears and building communication skills.

Source: www.magicme.co.uk

What can community development offer?

With its social justice goals, community development has worked to ensure that the arts are democratic and socially engaged. It develops inclusive processes that give people opportunities to have their own creative voice but also to make connections and work collectively. The process is as important as the product. The community development literature provides many different examples of the ways in which this is done.

Community festivals and carnivals are powerful expressions of community identity. They offer opportunities for the expression and celebration of different cultural identities. They may contain many different elements, involving local people as individuals, schools and clubs in performance, costume and exhibition design and building parade floats, as well as simply offering a space for people to come together. They are an opportunity to celebrate the diversity within a community.

Community theatre has been used to tell the history of an area, involving large parts of the community – again often through schools and local associations. It may be used to recreate local history, to engage different parts of the community in discussion about issues of local concern or to highlight these issues to the wider community or external actors. Alternatively, local theatres may set up outreach projects to reach people in nearby public housing estates who would not normally go near a theatre. In the global South, participatory forum theatre is used to galvanise community action and for education purposes (Boal, 2008).

There are many examples in the literature of young people engaging through music, through video production or through setting up local radio stations. This gives them skills, takes their voices into a wide arena and challenges stereotypes. Local home-grown media also challenge the hegemony of the globalised media and corporate branding and help to cement local identity. Arts activities also attract outsiders. A music and dance summer school in a socially and economically depressed rural area gave a new focus to the community, bringing resources and visitors into the area.

Box 6.8   Engaging young people

In a village in North Devon, young people who were often seen as a nuisance by local residents made a video about what it was like to live in a small coastal town where there was very little for them to do. The video was shown far and wide – the young people even went to London to show it to central government ministers. They formed an association to campaign for a skateboard park and several of them became part of the government's Young Advisors scheme, regularly consulted by policy makers on youth policy.

Photojournalism is another way in which local people can be given a voice and an opportunity to express their views about local life and the local environment. Exhibiting the photos provides an opportunity to compare different perceptions.

Murals can brighten up a neighbourhood and express community identity. Graffiti walls can engage young people and turn a problem into an asset. Children in one estate designed the new security gates, turning a negative into a positive asset.

Museums might work with the local community to bring to life local history projects. Local history has also been a focus of writing projects. Community centres could employ a writer or artist in residence to work with local people.

Crafts organisations can create a democratic space for participants to discuss matters of local concern – quilting, for example, has provided opportunities for local debate as well as making a strong democratic statement to the outside world.

Challenges

Community arts work is versatile. In terms of the outcomes that policy makers are looking for, it can tick a lot of boxes, contributing to education achievement and physical improvements, and sometimes bringing jobs into the community. But developing community arts can be a tough call. A special issue of the *Community Development Journal* (vol 42, no 4) warns that the globalised media can have a devastating effect on traditional forms of culture and practice. It also underlines the tendency for art and cultural activity to bolster dominant ideologies. It warns against treating community arts activities as remedial, with patronising attitudes towards anything that is produced.

The literature also highlights the dangers of commodification and exploitation. There are obvious ironies in the fact that graffiti – the art of the ghetto – is now itself the subject of glossy coffee table books rather than challenging the consumer economy. An English graffiti artist – Banksy – is now listed as one of the world's top 500 influential people and his works sell for vast sums.

Arts work needs to create opportunities for dialogue, debate and exploration if it is to serve community development goals. But arts activity is not necessarily concerned with social change and may be a panacea rather than addressing the root causes of social problems. And while it may get people involved, it is prey to the pitfalls of any other kind of community development: images may be divisive as well as inclusive.

A successful arts enterprise may not touch large parts of the community. Artists can be solitary creatures and persuading them to work in a collegial way – where the ideas come up from local communities rather than from the artist – can be difficult. There is also a huge culture clash between the artistic world and the managerialism required of funded community work projects. Finally, in times when resources are scarce, there is a need for robust evaluation. The impact of arts work is as hard to measure as any other form of community development.

Brief conclusion

The sections in this chapter demonstrate that community development – as a broad-based, holistic approach that starts from people's own concerns – can contribute to many different policy areas, supporting community participation and community solutions. But because it is a generic practice, it is not confined to particular policy areas, and this is apparent from the links in the earlier sections between community arts, environmental and educational work, for example, or between housing, economic development and regeneration work.

Summary

- Community development contributes to effective working in a range of policy areas.
- It enables professionals to identify and respond to community priorities in services and planning.
- Community development enhances participation, especially in relation to those groups that are more difficult to engage.
- For many service providers, community development poses some challenges in relation to decision making which they are not always equipped to handle.

Further reading

Each of the policy areas described here has its own specialist literature but *Critical community practice* (Butcher et al, 2007) provides an excellent introduction to the general techniques and challenges. The recent OECD publication, *Community capacity building* (edited by Noya, Clarence and Craig), brings together examples of effective practice from around the world, with specific chapters on health and regeneration, the local economy and environmental justice. Chris Church has written extensively on community-led approaches to sustainable development, and the Community Development Foundation has produced recent research reports on working with migrant, faith and refugee communities. LEAP for health (www.evaluationsupportscotland.org.uk/article.asp?id=62) sets out how community development techniques can be applied in this field and the Scottish Community Health Exchange has a range of publications, including a newsletter. Marj Mayo is an expert of the application of community development to community-based education, including a recent edited book (2008b) on active learning for active citizenship and the *Community Development Journal* has produced a special issue on community arts (vol 42, no 4). Over many years now, the Joseph Rowntree Foundation has been publishing research-based books on using community involvement to tackle regeneration, poverty and other policy areas.

7

challenges for practice

This guide has identified a number of challenges for community development to address, but there are also intrinsic tensions within community development practice to which there are no easy answers. These are the subject of ongoing debate whose solutions need to reflect local conditions and relationships.

As a form of intervention, community development has found itself located in different agencies and different departments within local authorities, sometimes at the heart of the hierarchy, more often on the edges or within a specialist team. Community development has often struggled to survive. Its purpose is constantly contested and revisited, and it is frequently resourced through short-term projects, fragmented funding and precarious job contracts. And yet it has been constantly rediscovered by policy makers and public service managers seeking to increase community involvement or to reach the most marginalised people in society (Mayo, 2008).

The methods and values of community development make it indispensible, while at the same time, practitioners experience a number of tensions and dilemmas that arise because of their role and commitments. The situations they find themselves in are rarely straightforward and in fact are often characterised by ambiguity, sometimes generating conflicting loyalties and 'role strain' (Hoggett et al, 2009). This chapter explores some of these challenges and makes recommendations about how they might be addressed.

Orientation

Previous chapters have illustrated how community development is often crucial in spanning the boundary between communities and the state, as well as working across other sectoral or community divisions. As a consequence, some critics have argued that community development has allowed itself to become co-opted into the government's agenda, losing its room to manoeuvre and criticise (Pitchford, 2008; Craig, 2011). Community development is commonly state-sponsored in that workers are either employed directly by local authorities, or their money comes via government grants. A perennial dilemma for community development workers arises from their role in supporting communities to tackle issues that they perceive as important, and to do this in ways that are responsive to people's needs while building capacity at the same time. This is intrinsic to all definitions of community development and yet most posts are funded by organisations that have their own agendas and priorities. Their objectives need to be achieved and the workers are answerable to their employers. A recent survey of workers in the UK indicated that the majority of community development workers are managed by people who do not have a background in or basic understanding of community development principles (Sender et al, 2010).

This creates particular difficulties if the projects that the community favours are not in accordance with agency objectives or seem likely to mature too slowly for the timescales imposed by a regime of performance targets. An experienced worker will understand this tension, explain it to all parties and negotiate a way forward that is in accordance with community wishes but also satisfies their employers. Less experienced workers often find it hard to manage this tension and may capitulate to their manager's demands (or else resign).

In recent years, community development has become drawn into strategies for community engagement and empowerment. Statutory agencies have quite rightly recognised the contribution that community development makes to effective participatory democracy (Bowles, 2008) but have not always taken on board the *primary* orientation of the workers, which is towards communities and civil society, rather than the state. Community development is fundamentally concerned with power relations, in society at large and at the micro level. It is inevitable therefore that workers may find themselves caught in conflicts between those who hold power and those who want or deserve more influence over the conditions of their lives. Dealing with tensions and trouble is endemic to effective practice, and yet not all practitioners have the experience or skills to do this, preferring to suppress conflict rather than devising strategies for resolving it equitably. Developing the personal and collective capacities for mediating conflicts is a neglected aspect of modern community development (Craig, cited in Shaw, 2004).

Status and recognition

There has been a long-running debate in community development over whether it should be seen as a profession (with all the attendant restrictions regarding entry qualifications and standards) or whether it is more like a social movement, drawing on a network of activists, some of whom are lucky enough to be paid for their work with communities. The latter position reflects community development's rejection of notions of expertise or elitism, and a well-intentioned desire to acknowledge people of all backgrounds for their community development work. Those who take the stance that community development should claim the status of a profession argue that it is an occupation requiring specialist knowledge, sophisticated judgements and dedicated effort, at a level at least equivalent to the work of other recognised professions such as a social work, planning or teaching. Unless community development is understood as a skilled and strategic intervention, it will be seen as amateurish and peripheral to mainstream work, while without proper training and management support, it is in danger of being poorly practised and losing its value base.

However, there is always a risk that being 'too' professional can be intimidating or off-putting for community members. Community development workers can be seen as representing authority or bringing expertise to the group and this may generate deference or antagonism, which can get in the way of working with communities in ways that value *their* skills and opinions.

As a result of this unresolved ambivalence, community development continues to be poorly resourced, receiving sporadic support from policy makers and politicians and often relying on the enthusiasm of individual officers or civil servants to ensure that it is even mentioned in reports or policy statements. There is urgent need for community development to be much more firmly embedded across a whole range of programmes relating to health, well-being, social inclusion, civil renewal and community enterprise.

Role boundaries

It would help if community development workers were more explicit about their role in relation to enabling community members to take action, to find their voice or to make links with others. This is different from being a member, representative or leader of the community, but this distinction is not always clearly drawn and indeed sometimes denied. Many community development workers are drawn to the role from a basis of activism in their own communities, determined to improve life for their families, neighbours and the community to which they feel they belong, which turns into a more generalised aspiration to promote greater equality and empowerment, for example for working class people (Hoggett et al, 2009). They may be driven by compassion or solidarity, possibly framed by human rights or faith perspectives, and this subjective involvement in the work will affect both priorities and direction of progress. It also seems to provide a form of personal conviction that Hoggett and colleagues term self-authorisation, enabling people to be both partisan and professional in resolving practice dilemmas that arise from the conflicting interests and social identities that characterise community life.

This is not to say that community development workers must be distant or objective, merely that they are aware of the boundaries around their role and do not inadvertently pursue their own objectives. In chapter two of her book, Gilchrist (2009) refers to the 7 Es of community development. These, were devised to highlight the ways in which the workers are helping *others* to grow, organise and learn, rather than promoting their own interests or needs.

Community belonging: place and identity?

Communities are traditionally regarded as consisting of 'local' people living or working in a particular locality. Community development is generally organised around area teams or by associating a worker with a 'neighbourhood', often of indeterminate size and boundaries. It is presumed that residents will want to organise or speak out as a local community, to improve the quality of life in 'their' area. This was probably a reasonable assumption in the days when people lived, worked, played, socialised, worshipped and learnt together within a few square miles, with plenty of opportunities for regular interaction between neighbours and workmates. However, in the last few decades, lives have become more fluid and many of us identify with several communities, each relating to different aspects of our lives. Areas differ enormously in how much they resemble the 'close-knit' communities of imagined yesteryear, and the neighbourhoods where community workers are found are mostly places where many residents have not actively chosen to live and yet they usually manage to sustain strong allegiances and a necessary sense of community spirit. Other areas function as little more than commuter dormitories where there is little sense of place as a unifying bond, with residents rarely meeting and often not even knowing the names of their next-door neighbours.

Where communities do organise locally, this may be as part of an externally imposed government initiative targeted at their 'zone' or in response to a threat or perceived intrusion, such as a proposal to locate a Travellers' site nearby. There are frequent examples of NIMBY-ism (not in my backyard), where communities unite against incinerators or plans for a new housing estate. Similarly, attempts to provide hostels or sheltered accommodation for people associated with stigma or crimes (such as people with learning difficulties, on bail or recovering from addiction) are known to generate hostility and fear. This kind of low-level neighbourhood-ism poses dilemmas for the community worker, who on the one hand is supposed to support communities on issues that they identify, while on the other hand, is also guided by values around treating marginalised people with respect and compassion.

Many of the problems experienced by communities are symptomatic of wider structural issues arising from the (global) economy, patterns of migration or government policies. They cannot be solved at local level through projects and relatively short-term interventions. As we saw in Chapter Four, this was the critique first expressed by the Community Development Projects set up in target neighbourhoods in the 1970s. The focus on localism and neighbourhood activities apparent in today's government policy may present community development with both opportunities and challenges. In particular, it will be vital for communities to connect above the local level, so as to understand and tackle the root causes of their problems, which may well be located far away and influenced by a distant set of political levers.

Not everyone chooses to engage with local community interests. For many, the most significant aspect of their lives may reflect an aspect of their identity that they want to keep private due to continuing social stigma or simply because it is not shared by their immediate neighbours. So, for example, a refugee family from Sierra Leone might reasonably prefer to construct their community around fellow West Africans living in this country, and be absorbed in campaigns for better HIV services. Others may associate more frequently with people who share a hobby, such as a Viking reconstruction society, knitting or fellow football supporters, spending their leisure time away from home and not taking much interest in their place of residence.

People who experience particular forms of discrimination are also more likely to use that identity to make connections with others in similar predicaments – either because they feel safer or to organise to change things (or both). Black and minority ethnic people have been effective in establishing community and voluntary organisations as well as faith bodies that provide important points of focus for the different communities and the core of vital alliances against racism. This approach, sometimes termed the 'radical pluralism of identity politics' (Hoggett et al, 2009, p 20), has provided some important threads for community development, especially in very diverse settings where resources are tight. There is good evidence that members of minority communities who have a strong sense of identity and feel secure in their 'home' cultures are more likely to integrate with the wider population. This is a persuasive argument for supporting the setting up of identity-based organisations which can run activities and specialist services that are appropriate for different ethnicities and faiths, ensuring that there is equality of provision as well as opportunities for building social capital. However, this has been challenged by some politicians and policy makers, who assert that 'single-identity' funding (as it has been called) encourages divisions between communities and undermines the cohesion of society. For community development, the challenge is to acknowledge the intersectionality of people's identities (the interaction of different aspects of their lives) and find ways of supporting people to organise around their preferred issues and interests (Gilchrist et al, 2010).

Equality and diversity

Campaigning for equalities and self-proclaimed identities often go hand-in-hand. As we saw in Chapter Two, equality is a core value for community development but nonetheless it can be difficult to work out what is fair in any given situation. There are historical factors to consider in the way that people have been treated in the past that continues to result in disadvantage; for example, the segregated schools system for children with hearing impairments meant that Deaf adults did not receive the same quality of education. Failure to understand or respect different cultural requirements, such as halal food, can exclude people from accessing services such as elder care.

Community development is concerned with all such issues and has developed a certain level of expertise in tackling discrimination and prejudice using what are sometimes known collectively as positive action measures (Gilchrist, 2007). These include making sure that the things that deter people from participating in community activities or prevent them from making use of opportunities or services are identified and tackled. For example, it may be necessary to produce posters or pamphlets in more than one language or to use positive images of minority groups in publicity material to indicate that the event is open to everyone. Some people are worried about going out at night to attend evening meetings, so it might be a good idea to have day time gatherings occasionally or to arrange transport. If people expect hostility or ridicule, they may prefer to meet separately, for example as a group of older lesbians, instead of engaging in more mainstream activities. Others may need help with their caring responsibilities, perhaps by providing a crèche or money to cover short-term respite.

Implementing such measures with limited funding might be difficult and can lead to accusations of favouritism or bias towards 'equality groups'. This is often resented by people who feel that they are also at a disadvantage or who believe in 'treating everyone the same'. Community development workers who are proactive in tackling inequalities may find themselves criticised. They need to be careful to justify their work with certain groups and to make sure that they cannot be accused of looking after their own interests, especially if they share the same identity, for example as a woman. Dealing with cultural insensitivity and prejudicial attitudes can be challenging. Somehow the practitioners or organisation must strike a balance between being supportive towards community members and explaining why certain language or behaviour is regarded as derogatory or exclusive. It is by no means straightforward to simultaneously ensure inclusivity, diversity and equality in one's work, while seeking to promote community empowerment!

The pan-equalities framework has been developed over the past decade and is now enshrined in the 2010 Equality Act. It is based on a different model for understanding how people come to be disadvantaged, taking an integrated approach to the different equality strands by looking at what factors restrict the chances of people fulfilling their 'capabilities' in life (based on Sen, 2009). In many instances, disadvantage is correlated with biological features, such as sex, age, skin colour and so on, which render people vulnerable to discrimination or restrict their choices. Other factors are more socially determined, such as those prejudices associated with faith, sexual orientation or class background. Different factors tend to interact in people's lives such that an older professional mother, perhaps with grown-up children, is less likely to be turned down for a job than a younger Asian women of childbearing age, who may suffer from both sexist and racist assumptions about her employability. The pan-equalities approach has been criticised by some equalities communities, who argue that it marginalises the social impact of widespread disadvantage affecting whole populations, focusing instead on the experience and capabilities of individuals. For community development, it allows flexibility in promoting equality in opportunities and outcomes at a local level in specific circumstances, as well as tackling more pervasive biases and barriers that discourage participation of some sections of the community.

Leadership issues

Building the capacity of communities and enabling people to organise collectively means thinking about how leadership operates and how it can be nurtured. Paradoxically, community leaders are not always the best people to champion community interests, even though they may be hard-working and articulate. Their role can sometimes put them at odds with other members of the community that they purport to represent. This can be for a variety of reasons. They may have got caught up in partnership arrangements, devoting lots of spare time to committees and leaving little energy to keep in touch with what ordinary residents want. Or they may be too partisan, interested only in narrow issues or obtaining resources for their favourite groups. A common difficulty arises when leaders are unwilling to delegate aspects of their role to others or to hand over the reins altogether. This can result in burn-out and stagnation. Community development can encourage community leadership that reflects both the population concerned and its own values. In other words, it tries to ensure a style of leadership that is inclusive, collaborative, egalitarian and democratic.

This model, in which power and responsibilities are more distributed within a group, contrasts with what is understood as 'good leadership' in other spheres, where the emphasis might be on individual characteristics, such as charisma, decisiveness and single-mindedness. Community development therefore needs to create conditions where the best leaders can emerge through debate and action, so that they can build a consensus among members, represent or articulate their views, and work with others to turn ideas into action. A recent model of 'liberating leadership' proposes four essential elements: describing it as 'a process of inspiring, supporting, *working with* and *influencing others* in a group, team, organisation or community, based on an *agreed set of principles*, to achieve *common goals* and social change' (Skinner and Farrar, 2009; emphasis added). Sometimes it is necessary to challenge community leaders because they dominate discussion and are dismissive of ideas that don't match their own. This may not be easy for community members to do themselves, perhaps because of the leader's status or because of misguided loyalty. Community workers can be more objective and possibly more diplomatic, suggesting alternative ways of looking at a situation or encouraging other potential leaders to put themselves forward or to pursue a different course of action. Their role may be to 'hold the ring' while disputes and discussions play out, ensuring that issues are dealt with fairly and civilly.

Unfortunately, what communities want is not always right or legal and people can act in selfish, prejudiced and defensive ways that exacerbate division and discrimination, rather than fostering community spirit and equality. Individual activists and community leaders may dominate discussions because they are articulate, loud or able to give the most time. This can drown out the quieter, less confident voices, masking or distorting their opinions and potentially misrepresenting the communities' views. Although community workers can be guilty of these tendencies too, the challenge for the person working with such communities is twofold: firstly, to build the capacity to debate difficult issues and manage competing interests; secondly, to ensure that the more obscure or uncomfortable perspectives are able to influence decisions, perhaps by acting on their when the are or finding other routes for them to be heard. Active citizens can be awkward citizens, sometimes showing an 'ugly' face that can be intimidating or cynical, but nevertheless, locally committed and enterprising. Although they may have preferences, workers cannot pick and choose who they work with in a group and must find ways to enable people to collaborate constructively with one another and with decision makers.

There is a balance to be struck between involving the 'usual suspects' and finding fresh new voices who supply alternative perspectives and challenges. On the one hand it is helpful to develop and harness the continuity and expertise that participation brings, but it also vital that these people are able to genuinely represent a full range of community views. This is why accountability is so important for communities and practitioners alike.

Accountability

Community development is often shaped by a complex array of formal and informal accountabilities and workers can easily be pulled in different directions. Their employer expects them to adhere to organisational policies and priorities. Their manager, usually closer to the specific aims of the work, will want to see progress towards these. Funders, for example a charitable foundation, will usually have their own set of goals or projects, to which they in turn are answerable to donors. Community members tend to want the worker to be responding to their immediate needs: organising events, running a group, sorting out troublesome committees, raising money and so on. Meanwhile practice is supposed to conform to those values and principles established by the field of peers and professionals, notably around participation, empowerment, learning and equality. In other words, community workers are to assist and enable communities, not simply do things for them. As a result, incongruities may emerge in terms of other people's expectations regarding the pace, the processes and even the direction of the work.

Issues of accountability are further compounded for workers employed by elected authorities such as district or county councils. The tensions between representative and participative democracy are inherent in the electoral system that sees councillors as community leaders and yet desires active engagement of communities in public decision making processes and service delivery. Community development has been drawn ever more deeply into the empowerment agenda, helping authorities to set up engagement structures and to be more strategic in their work with communities. Consequently, many workers report that they have become embroiled in council bureaucracy and are losing their involvement with grassroots activists.

As Chapter Six has demonstrated, it has never been that clear who 'owns' community development and this confusion continues to this day. In the past, community development has been located in education departments (alongside youth work), as part of 'patch' social work teams, within health services, regeneration programmes (fostering local economic development and social enterprise) and most recently embedded in community engagement units, often based in a central department accountable to the chief executive. Public service spending cuts have rendered these latter posts especially vulnerable.

Mainstreaming, targeted or specialist work?

It could be argued that the profile of community development has been strengthened by the extent to which it has been recognised as a way of working that increases empowerment and improves engagement; this has also made its methods available to a wider range of professions (Chanan and Miller, 2009). However, the mainstreaming of community development has not allowed it to prove its worth as an effective way of tackling deep-rooted problems. Unfortunately its skills and values appear to have become diluted, reduced to a set of techniques captured in a bewildering array of toolkits and guides.

It is assumed that everyone who works with communities or even just works in a community setting is doing community development and yet, as we set out in Chapter Two, there is an acknowledged repertoire of skills, values and roles that characterise effective and inclusive practice.

Somehow community development still needs to present convincing evidence that it offers a specialist service, particularly in relation to reaching target groups who are 'under-served' and 'seldom heard' by mainstream providers. Community development comes into its own when working in deprived neighbourhoods or with particularly disadvantaged groups, but it is an approach that would benefit all communities, helping them to avoid or deal with many of the issues that occur when volunteers or small community groups come together to deliver services or influence wider decisions.

Demonstrating impact: measuring the social return

By its nature, community development tends to operate behind the scenes and often in conjunction with a number of other partners, not least community members themselves. It is inherently difficult to predict what is going to happen and how or when the benefits will appear because there are many people involved, often on a voluntary basis, who are accountable to a range of bodies or sometimes to no one at all. Furthermore, progress depends on a range of factors, most of which are not in the control of either the community or the community development workers. For example, a successful event might be dependent on obtaining funding, good weather, a favourable vote on the Council or having a sufficient number of volunteers turning up.

Community development claims to improve the quality of life for people, especially disadvantaged groups, by helping them to engage with services, increase their influence over decision making and generally lead healthier, happier lives. Statutory employers of community development workers usually expect evidence that intervention plans have been delivered and that things have improved in line with their policy goals or nationally imposed targets, for example in relation to educational attainment or employment. Modern managerialism, an approach that came to prominence in the 1990s, adopted a model of linear progress that could be measured through preplanned outputs and the achievement of specified targets. Some managers of community development strategies imagine that the performance of their teams can be monitored in this way but fail to take into account the complexity of the work. Nor do they understand that community development is primarily concerned with the issues that communities decide are important and the strategies that they identify as meeting their needs (Miller, 2008). In these circumstances it is simply not feasible to plan and predict detailed objectives. In fact, too much focus on predetermined targets would reduce the responsiveness inherent in good community development. Communities change their collective minds about what they want to achieve and which issues they want to prioritise. Their aspirations evolve over time as they learn from their own successes and the experiences of others. The funding and policy context also shapes the feasibility of different options, so community workers need to be alert and flexible in their approach.

Nevertheless, if community development is to be taken seriously as a professional intervention, then it must be able to show what difference it makes for communities and how this delivers desired policy and social outcomes. There are several recognised models for evaluating the work, with perhaps the most ubiquitous being the ABCD (Achieving Better Community Development) framework (Barr and Hashagen, 2000). This was originally devised by the Scottish Community Development Centre and has been extensively used and refined, most recently to become the planning and evaluation toolkit, LEAP. It takes as its starting point an ideal vision of a strong and empowered community that is liveable, sustainable and equitable. This translates into five quality of life dimensions around shared wealth, caring, safety, creativity and citizenship. These in turn are supported by four building blocks of personal empowerment, positive action, community organisation and participation. The challenge in terms of management is to identify the performance criteria that can be used to assess the community development contribution towards implementing these. There are many examples of toolkits designed to assess progress, but very few that are based on communities defining goals for themselves.

Professional standards and ethics

In Chapter Two, we emphasised that community development can best be seen as a set of principles that govern the processes of working towards social change and collective capacity building. A major challenge for community development continues to revolve around the balance between *how* the work is done (that is, in accordance with community development values) and the accomplishment of specific goals. One guiding principle is to focus on improvements at community level, rather than individual rewards. Do people generally have less fear of crime? Does the refurbished village hall act as a community anchor building? Are relations between young people and the older generation more cordial and respectful? Have incidents of racial harassment declined? There should be shared gains, although individuals directly involved will almost certainly benefit more because of their enhanced skills, confidence, networks and opportunities. Sometimes, however, there can be a tension between what individuals want and what might seem best for the wider community. Just as in the case of flawed leadership, community development workers are regularly faced with conflicting interests that need resolving to everyone's satisfaction. Contrary to popular thinking, community is rarely about 'unity', and the principles of community development are not always able to give a clear indication of the best course of action. Practitioners need to think on their feet, using their discretion to make ethical and political judgements about what they should (or shouldn't) do.

The national occupational standards talk about 'appropriate practice' that conforms to a set of key values. Although they are not designed exclusively for professional community development workers, they provide a useful reference point for assessing whether a practitioner is acting within the roles of community development work. There are many routes into professional (paid) community development work, and an array of qualifications. While this can be seen as an advantage, opening doors for activists and volunteers, there needs to be coherent training provision and perhaps a body to regulate and validate qualifications at each level.

Brief conclusion

Community development faces many ways and has been harnessed for many purposes, not all of which sit comfortably with its espoused principles. Its emphasis on high-level, but often intangible outcomes such as community spirit or cohesion, has lent it a certain ambivalence about what it achieves on a day-to-day basis or through specific projects. Community development claims to tackle the causes of major social problems, but often makes little headway among the roots or becomes mired in dealing with the symptoms of poverty and conflict endemic in our unequal society. Only by maintaining a critical and reflexive praxis that links theory, politics and practice, will those engaged in community development work ensure that their efforts and skills make a difference to social justice in the long term (Shaw, 2004; Ledwith, 2005; Ledwith and Springett, 2010).

Community development is probably best regarded as an approach to social change that is carried out under many auspices by people in several different roles: the paid specialist community development worker, other professionals, social entrepreneurs, volunteers, community members, politically motivated activists, elected councillors and a whole range of people who simply want to make life better for individuals and communities, such as artists, faith leaders and school governors.

The ambiguities, dilemmas and challenges set out in this chapter reflect but also blur the core values and competences that define community development. As we will examine in the final chapter, its future is not clear and yet it draws on a tradition of practice and theory in the UK and across the world that will ensure its continuing relevance to social progress and democracy.

Summary

■ The status and purpose of community development is often obscured by political rhetoric and role ambiguity.
■ It is poorly recognised because it embodies processes that take time to mature and its impact is difficult to demonstrate among other changes at community level.
■ Community development works with communities of interest and these are often not tied to specific localities.
■ Work to promote equality and diversity is an important aspect of community development and poses a number of challenges.
■ Community development supports a shared model of leadership and is concerned with complex issues of representation and accountability.
■ Its value base provides a significant foundation for setting standards and guiding practice.

Further reading

The recent book, *The dilemmas of development work* (Hoggett et al, 2009) examines how practitioners operate in uncertain situations where their personal experience and values provide the necessary 'compass'. Pitchford's book (2008) poses important challenges for community development as a profession while making some key recommendations for future debate.

As mentioned in earlier chapters, national organisations such as the Community Development Exchange, the Federation for Community Development Learning and the Community Development Foundation are routes into interesting current debates and reflections on the state of community development in the UK.

8

current and future trends

This chapter considers likely trends in the external environment over the immediate future, what community development can offer in response to these trends and how they are likely to affect community development. It ends by asking what they mean for the evolution of community development as an occupation and approach in the coming years.

Back to the future?

At the beginning of this Short Guide, we commented on the high level of current interest in community development and other models of community practice across the political spectrum. Everyone seems to be looking for local, community-based solutions to the issues facing twenty-first century society. So where is this interest likely to lead us?

In 1979, the prospects for community development looked poor in the UK. The general election of that year took place against a background of cuts in public spending and rising unemployment. We were experiencing a new Conservative government committed to rolling back the state in favour of the market and civil society. In the 1980s, the labour movement and local authorities found themselves on the losing side of battles with central government. The response to urban deprivation was to be led by the private sector. In the US, Reaganomics was but two years away. In both countries, the gap between the rich and poor was starting to grow.

Despite this, in the subsequent years community development still found a place for a while, often supported in the UK by the 'new left' in local authorities opposed to the Thatcher regime. But at the end of the 1980s, as Chapter Three suggested, prospects again looked grim. Nonetheless, the pendulum was beginning to swing and in the early 1990s, with concern growing again about the fate of the most disadvantaged communities, new forms of partnership working were being introduced. In the UK, the introduction of the National Strategy for Neighbourhood Renewal at the turn of the century was an ambitious attempt to put communities, and by implication community development, at the heart of policies to tackle the deep-rooted and intractable problems of poverty and disaffection.

We are now in a position again where a right wing government has been elected against a background of financial crisis, with swingeing public spending cuts that could make those of the 1980s look like small change. But whereas for Margaret Thatcher, there was no such thing as society, now we have a government that is launching the Big Society. The US has a president of mixed heritage who spent significant years of his life as a community organiser in Chicago.

There are other differences. Sustainable development was still a minority interest at that time, although this was soon to change with the report of the Brundtland Commission in 1987 (World Commission on Environment and Development, 1987). The term 'climate change' was only just beginning to be used. Europe was still divided by the 'iron curtain'. Terrorism was certainly in the news – in Northern Ireland and Germany for example – but not dictating community policy to the extent it is now. In 1979, the mass use of mobile phones and web 2.0 technology was a very distant dream and although we lived in a global society, the benefits and otherwise of globalisation were not debated in the way they are today.

We do not intend in this final chapter to try to predict the future. Just a glance at the fate of past predictions suggests that this is a dangerous game. Nevertheless, as the short review earlier suggests, we can identify current trends in the external environment that present both dangers and opportunities for community development in 2010. These are:

■ the global economic crisis
■ the shrinking state
■ dynamic migration patterns and the changing significance of place
■ the digital age
■ sustainable development and climate change.

Global economic crisis: an opportunity for new sustainable models?

What does global economic crisis mean for community development? Can it be, as the Chinese proverb has it, both threat and opportunity? The first indications are fairly negative, insofar as the downturn has a disproportionate impact on the disadvantaged communities that are the focus of much community development work. It is widely anticipated that the poorest in society will suffer worst, especially those who are dependent on the public sector both for employment and for services that are now facing heavy cuts. Even under a boom economy, the gap between rich and poor widened. Current economic pressures will only reinforce trends which have concentrated the most vulnerable in society in the poorest housing, creating a spiral of disadvantage in terms of unemployment, poor health, poor educational attainment and so on. Indeed, as we go to press, commentators warn that UK cuts in housing benefit will displace many poorer families from the communities in which they now live. It remains to be seen how political protest, local social action and mass campaigns will evolve and be sustained over the coming years. Increasing hardship and inequalities may galvanise citizens of every background into collective organising; they might equally lead to growing community divisions and disaffection.

Pressure for survival may – as so many politicians hope – lead to self-help and new solidarities in poorer communities. But such pressures also tend to intensify competition within and between groups and fan resentments. Racial and generational tensions are familiar territory for community development, with their flames frequently fanned by the media. At the same time, the most disadvantaged areas become the repository for the social and environmental problems that no one else wants in their 'backyard'. Financial restructuring in the past has stripped the heart out of poorer communities and the operation of the market has left them without essential resources. On the one hand, there is a strong rhetoric of localism in current policy that talks of bringing services closer to the people who need them; on the other, the market favours economies of scale, which work against this. Thus, while some in the UK advocate for the introduction here of the hugely important Community Reinvestment Act from the US[1] to address issues of financial exclusion and make banks more accountable locally for their investment decisions, the evidence is that the restructuring of the financial industry is leading to the loss of local banks (Blond, 2010).

Prospects for public funding at present look poor. Analysing the US War on Poverty in the 1960s, Peter Marris and Martin Rein (1967) argued that, in the medium and long term, there were no votes in initiatives or policies to help the most disadvantaged in society. The same is likely to apply in countries like the UK. And funds for activities whose outcomes do not conform to helpful political timescales are highly vulnerable (Wind-Cowie, 2010). Equally precarious is funding for the voluntary and community sector. Over recent years, even decades, successive governments have invested in voluntary and community activity – a third of charitable income, for example, comes from statutory sources. Now cuts in public spending threaten this investment. Over recent years, government has also invested in the infrastructure for this activity, the support services at national, regional and local level that are particularly important for small community groups with few resources of their own. This too is at risk, along with the posts within public bodies that have supported community and voluntary sector development over the years. As this book goes to press, high-profile commentators are warning that cuts of this magnitude will fatally undermine the very Big Society that the coalition government is seeking to build.

There are those who believe that community development has become too dependent on public sector funding, however. Some have argued for years that this dependency compromises its independence, and that this is also compromised by its engagement in the 'invited spaces' of government-led partnerships. Organisations such as London Citizens in the UK and the Industrial Areas Foundation in the US, for example, are demonstrating what can be done without state funding, through the resources of faith communities, schools and other organisations, such as the trade unions. Retrenchment, for critics of government funding, may well allow community development to rediscover its political soul.

Even if it is not cut, the likelihood is that community development funding from any public or other institutional source will in the future be expected to produce efficiency savings – through preventing problems and easing demand on public services, for example. There may well be scope for streamlining in some parts of the community sector, for example through mergers. However, efficiencies will need to be defined in radically different ways from those in some other parts of the economy. Work to explore ways of capturing social returns on investment has been going on for some time and, while it has yet to deliver on its promise, there is considerable potential here for building the business case for community development. More needs to be done to show how accounting for social value can be made to work in practice, and to test and consolidate innovative ideas in this field. In the meantime, it will be important to ensure that competition for scarce funding does not inhibit cooperation in the search for more creative solutions.

Maybe a more positive outlook comes from what one commentator (Karl Wilding, personal communication) calls a 'relentless search for social (financial) innovation'. Successive UK governments have proposed bringing dormant bank accounts into use, although this involves substantial challenges. There has also been considerable policy interest in what a leading UK think tank calls 'recapitalising the poor' (see www.demos.co.uk). It is unclear, as yet, what this will entail. The sale of council housing, for example, may have recapitalised some of the poor, but its side effects meant that the stock for those without this choice was significantly reduced. The call from the left of the political spectrum would be for a more fundamental redistribution of wealth, but the lesson from history across the globe so far is that, even under governments committed to some form of redistribution, this has failed to materialise.

As we saw in earlier chapters, recent UK policy has promoted the transfer of public sector assets to communities. Putting assets into the hands of poorer communities – whether they are individual or collective – enables them to ride the crisis and be more flexible in solving their problems. Of course, this is most likely to work if assets transferred are useful and wanted, with a genuine potential to raise revenue to run them, and not liabilities in a poor state of repair.

The current interest in social enterprise offers another way forward, as we saw in Chapter Six. Again there are well-documented pitfalls, especially where the need to raise money on the private market trumps the social bottom line. The experience of the social housing sector in the UK demonstrates the challenges in this respect. Here, the need to attract market finance has led to increasing economies of scale. Mergers and consolidation have led to increasing centralisation among UK voluntary housing associations, which, like community development corporations in the US, have also been criticised for behaving more and more like private enterprises.

This is not inevitable. While there are challenges, there are also positive lessons from the considerable experience of enterprise and asset ownership to date. The Scottish community-based housing association movement retains its roots while the growth of the development trusts movement in the UK over recent years also offers more positive stories. There are also a host of examples of ordinary people using their initiative, local resources and knowledge of community markets to set up cooperatives and community enterprises that are innovative and income generating, and meet definite social needs. Growing a business that can generate income for reinvestment requires determination and support – social investment is still a drop in the ocean. Nonetheless, increased interest in sustainable development and social innovation, along with the search for new economic models, may offer promising signs for the future.

Community development can contribute a great deal to this agenda. It can support groups in assessing whether to take up opportunities to engage in enterprise and take on assets, so that they can make informed decisions. It can also pass on the lessons from past experience. If communities are to gain the maximum advantage of these opportunities, community development workers will also need to engage with leading thinking on this front and with innovative entrepreneurs, exploring ways of working creatively with private business and new financial arrangements like social impact bonds. But community development will also have an important role to play in monitoring the impact of new developments on all parts of the community and ensuring that groups who pursue this agenda remain firmly rooted in, and accountable to, their foundations in the community.

The shrinking state: preserving the public sphere

The state is the fall guy in much political rhetoric today. But in a decade when many governments are committed to reducing the role of the state, can communities take on all the responsibilities demanded of them, especially communities already under pressure? A world where civil society reigns unchecked is unlikely to be the romantic utopia its advocates imagine. The mediating hand of the state is needed to balance competing interests, support the unorganised, ensure accountability and so on. The rolling back of the state also presents a challenge to many community development workers – at least in advanced democracies – who see it as the ultimate guarantor of equalities and social justice.

The promise of more powers to communities is in essence one we should welcome. Certainly this is a prospect that will be attractive to many at local level. However, it does come with a number of health warnings. One is that resources are not evenly distributed. A number of studies over the years have shown volunteering to be higher in affluent than in low income neighbourhoods. Low income neighbourhoods will therefore be doubly disadvantaged. There are dangers, also referred to in earlier chapters, that communities will be set up to fail, expected to take on services and assets that others have failed to provide or manage successfully, without being afforded adequate resources and guidance.

The fragmentation of service delivery in the hands of a growing variety of providers and procurers will also raise major questions about accountability. The contracting out of services already means that it is more and more difficult to know who to hold responsible when things go wrong. Paradoxically, transferring delivery from the state to non-profit organisations can lead to more rather than less centralised control, as the theorists in Chapter Four argued. Commentators lament the increase in regulation that has accompanied state funding in recent years. This is partly in order to maintain parity across areas and to protect service users, especially those most vulnerable to abuse. But this increased regulation has hit communities hard as they find themselves struggling to implement health and safety regulations, criminal checks and burdensome monitoring schemes as well as to escape an increasingly litigious society and a media waiting to pounce on any infringement. This regime of 'red tape' puts off all but the most determined volunteers.

There may be good initial reasons behind all of these measures, but the unintended consequences are considerable. Most men, for example, will need to think very hard nowadays before volunteering to work with children. Volunteers may be put off by the need to obtain the necessary certificates for food hygiene standards before being allowed to run a jam and cake stall to raise money for their local good cause. Corporations meanwhile resist regulation and are notoriously difficult to hold to account. Insofar as litigation has replaced traditional forms of accountability, it has created an increasingly risk-averse society and is in any case not a realistic option for the poorest and most disenfranchised in society. Class actions, for example, are difficult to pursue under UK law.

If this seems unduly negative, the examples in previous chapters tell the story of how much can be achieved by community development, often in partnership with or with the support of the state. Moves towards co-production – at individual and community level – offer new opportunities that allow communities to contribute to the production of local goods and services as they see fit. There are also very positive examples of community-run services to learn from and we can also learn from the failures of the past. Distilling and applying these lessons is something that community workers are well placed to do, helping to ensure that community-run services are appropriate, responsive, inclusive and accountable.

Helping communities to make their voices heard when services are threatened or do not meet their needs will also continue to be a priority, through finding creative ways of holding services and other external actors to account, especially for those in communities whose needs are not adequately or appropriately met. Community audit is an idea that is emerging in a number of circles and could provide an imaginative alternative to top-down regulation, especially with the demise of the Audit Commission.

Some argue that it is not only the state that is shrinking but the whole of the public sphere. Physical public spaces where people could mix with people unlike themselves are now privatised or felt to be unsafe. Community centres, open access leisure and sports facilities, adult education, public parks and libraries are likely to suffer further from the cuts. We also commented earlier on the disappearance of the traditional spaces where citizens could debate public issues and learn political skills at local level. We cannot return to the past – and, in any case, some of these institutions had their own failings. But community development needs to take on the challenge of creating new gathering places – new spaces for dialogue and debate in and across the most disadvantaged communities.

As part of its Big Society drive, the UK government intends to train an army of community organisers. This is welcome insofar as it recognises the need to support community development, although there are questions of resourcing to be resolved – currently they are expected to become self-financing. To an extent, this initiative draws on the success of organisations like London Citizens in capturing the attention of policy makers, which demonstrates how different communities can be brought together around common issues and it may bode well for community development in the future.

Significantly, as outlined in Chapter Two, community organising provides a model which combines activities and services on the ground with highly successful advocacy and campaigning strategies, something which communities are not always able to do successfully on their own. This advocacy role will be essential in the face of the economic challenges we discussed in the previous section.

Community organising is part of a radical tradition, drawing on the ideas of Saul Alinsky in the US in the mid-twentieth century. It remains to be seen whether the conflict strategies that he advocated are quite what the government had in mind. The demise of the Community Development Project and the US War on Poverty in the 1960s are salutary reminders of the fate of initiatives that take too seriously the commitment to give power back to the people. But there is a clear need in the twenty-first century to find new ways of understanding the notion of 'the public' and to reconfigure the relationship between state and citizen in ways that respond to twenty-first century aspirations and needs. If disadvantaged communities are not to be further excluded by such changes, community development will have an important role to play.

Redefining community: migration and its significance for place

Wars, climate change, the destruction of habitats, the global media, cheaper travel, the opening up of markets – all in their different ways have contributed to the movement of people over recent years.

However, while some borders have opened, others have closed. Anti-immigration moral panics illustrate the 'dark side' of community and responding with 'tough' policies on border control has always been an easy mark for politicians seeking popular support. The need to build bridges between suspicious communities will continue to provide a challenge for community development. But the shifting patterns of migration and settlement present some more fundamental challenges. In their discussion of the future for community development in the US, De Filippis and Saegert (2007) argue that immigration is transforming the meanings of both community and development, as communities become transnational. Thus, they ask whether, if a Mexican-American community pools money to build a community centre in its members' town of origin in Puebla, this contributes to community development in their home city of Chicago. Will the notion of community, as a result, become detached from place? If so, what will this mean for community development?

To announce the death of the local is premature. Localism is part of current political rhetoric and many commentators argue that place is still significant for most people, a view that is backed up by recent surveys. For disadvantaged communities with little bridging social capital, it is particularly important. But place is now one source of identity among many. Research has illustrated the complexity and ingenuity that people use to construct social identities. Identities are used strategically to create a sense of safety, to seek integration and to assert rights, for example in relation to sexual orientation or disability (Wetherell, 2009a, 2009b). Ethnic origin and citizenship are no longer straightforwardly aligned, leading to hybrid identities that combine nationality with other characteristics, such as British Muslim. Community development needs to take into account these more complicated patterns of belonging and be aware of the power differentials and political perspectives associated with them (Gilchrist et al, 2010).

New ways of knowing and communicating

It is a truism to say that digital technology has revolutionalised the way we live now, changing the way we access information and the way we communicate. It remains to be seen whether younger people, who have grown up with Web 2.0 and mobile phones, will understand notions of community, place, identity and organisation in the same ways as previous generations. As traditional public spaces disappear, will cyberspaces replace them? Young people are already 'hanging out' on social networking sites and interacting with friends mainly through SMS or Twitter. Will blogs replace the letters pages of local newspapers or public meetings in the village hall? The communications revolution has enabled globalisation from below, by giving communities in different parts of the world the means to communicate easily with each other. As the example given in the previous section illustrates, it has changed the meaning of community as it allows for instant communication between indigenous communities and their diasporic friends and family. Barack Obama's campaign for the US presidency demonstrated the power of community organising through new technology. It has also enabled the speedy organisation of global protest, disaster relief and the growth of independent media.

On a more local scale, digital technology has introduced new ways of mobilising people and made it possible to expand and strengthen local activity, by allowing virtual meetings to supplement face-to-face communication. Communities and citizens can access and share information on a scale unimagined in the early 1990s. Social networking sites allow groups to keep in touch with their members, let them know about their activities and mobilise support for campaigns. New virtual networks are being set up all the time to bring people together, keep communities in touch with each other and inform members about developments locally, nationally and across the globe. An increasing number of local websites operate as digital community newspapers (see, for example, www.Harringayonline.com), while sites such as Awaaz and Indymedia keep people in touch with national and international developments. There are many others.

Nothing comes without a price. There are downsides to this fantastic new resource. Perhaps the one that attracts most debate is the issue of digital exclusion. Those who are not on top of the latest developments risk losing left out and left behind. This is in part a question of access to resources, but new skills too are required, in filtering and retrieving information, in navigating perpetually changing technologies, in designing the message and its medium. Digital spaces are open to appropriation and surveillance by the powerful and to censorship. The advantages listed earlier carry their own risks too: information becomes ephemeral and vulnerable to manipulation; identities and loyalties too can become attenuated and fragmented, especially if they cease to be anchored off-line.

Community resources and skill sharing can help to combat problems of digital exclusion. There is a challenge for community development here in learning how to exploit the new technologies – and especially social networking – to nurture connections and complement face-to-face interaction. Nevertheless the evidence from research into local digital networks suggests that people use these extremely effectively to post information about community activities, to arrange face-to-face meetings with other residents and generally to maintain the foundations of community life.

Climate change and sustainable development

Chapter Six described the contribution that community development can make to the sustainable development challenge. As we saw there, the phrase 'think globally, act locally' originated in relation to environmental concerns. Recent extreme weather conditions remind us of the tremendous costs that will be – and are being – borne by communities; a sample for 2009–10 includes: the worst floods in Pakistan for 80 years; the hottest, driest weather in and around Moscow for 1,000 years; communities destroyed by wildfires in California and Australia; the heaviest rains in China for a decade causing mudslides with significant loss of life; and floods again on a lesser but unprecedented scale in many parts of Europe. Although nature is no respecter of class, it is still often the poorest communities that suffer most from environmental degradation and disaster or who end up with the industrial or waste processing facilities that are damaging to health and well-being.

We have commented earlier on the notion of community 'resilience'. The origins of this discourse lie in the field of disaster relief and prevention. The use of the term has since been applied to sustainable development and now to the economic challenges that face people in the poorest communities. This takes us back to where we began – the global economy. Indeed, the equitable distribution and preservation of the planet's resources – the triple (economic, social and environmental) bottom line – has been an important driver in the search for alternative economic forms and demonstrates the interrelatedness of the issues discussed here and elsewhere.

The challenge for community development is to convince communities that they have a role to play – that they can do something themselves. For while local 'clean and green' issues are often top of their agenda, the challenges of climate change often seem distant and beyond their control. Much larger forces are at work in causing climate change and environmental decay, but the search for solutions requires actions at every level, from global to very local.

Bringing it all together

We have reflected at several points in this Short Guide on the ways in which interest in and support for community development have ebbed and flowed over time. It has had to reinvent itself to suit political and ideological circumstances, and different models have come to the fore at different times and in different settings. Indeed this reinvention is reflected in debates about what language we should use to describe it. It has evolved a chameleon-like nature, which helps it to survive, but means that it can appear to take on the characteristics of other approaches or merge into the background and disappear altogether.

But this adaptability allows community development at best to take a holistic and flexible approach, placing it in a good position to help communities and those working with them to address the challenges of the future. The complexity of society today requires boundary spanners who can work, as John Gaventa (2003) put it, 'on both sides of the [power] equation'. This role requires particular strengths in dealing with competing demands and conflicting loyalties, but also in accepting that the boundary spanner will often be perceived as 'not one of us' by both sides, despite his or her best efforts (Howard and Taylor, 2010).

This takes us back to another of the debates we referred to in our Introduction – as to whether community development is an approach, a role, a profession or a movement. Over the decades, there have been fierce debates about values and the risk that these will be eroded if community development is used in an instrumental way or co-opted into government (or any other external) agendas. The sense of community development as a movement that was prevalent in the 1970s seems largely absent today, although some community development workers still resist professionalisation for this reason. At the other end of the spectrum, there is a feeling that community development needs to have some kind of professional identity if it is not to be watered down so far as to be seen as something anyone can do. It remains to be seen how further and higher education cuts will affect community development training.

There should be no contradiction between seeing community development as a movement with values, while at the same time demanding a professional and skilled approach. There will always be a spectrum of models and standards. But whatever the approach taken it is important that community development is embedded in a clear ethical framework and adopts a reflexive stance towards the dilemmas inherent in the work. As mentioned earlier, there were major debates in the 1960s and 1970s about whether community workers should be directive or non-directive. But this now seems a false dichotomy. Community development has a specific role in combining knowledge and ideas derived from the body of community development theory and practice over the decades with the experience and ideas of those it is working with in communities.

Summary

- The global economic crisis, coupled with a reduction of the role of the state, is likely to hit the poorest communities particularly hard. Climate change is also likely to have the greatest impact on the poorest communities.
- Community development has a role in the development of new and sustainable local economic approaches, in supporting communities to run their own services and public spaces and in exploring new forms of co-production.
- If these are to work for all parts of the community, community development needs to retain its role in supporting community voice, to protect the resources and services these communities can ill afford to lose, to hold new types of provision accountable and to work with allies to tackle the external factors which hold these communities back.
- Community development will also need to build on its boundary spanning role, working with new providers and decision makers from all sectors to make services work with and for local people.
- Community development will need to acknowledge and work with new kinds of communities as changing migration patterns and the digital age change the meaning of collective identities and, maybe, weaken the significance of locality.
- As the public sphere shrinks, community development also has an important role in creating new spaces for dialogue and democratic debate.
- New technologies create exciting new opportunities for communication and public debate but, like most magic bullets, they have their pitfalls. Community development cannot afford to be left behind in this revolution or in understanding its implications.
- Community development's adaptability will be at a premium in meeting new external challenges. But it needs to be embedded in a strong ethical framework and understanding of the skills and values needed to work for social justice in the poorest communities.

Further reading

For an understanding of current and future trends, readers need to go to the web. The think tanks are the place to go for research on new opportunities and trends. Forum for the Future provides a particularly useful summary of 'weak signals' – examples of new debates and initiatives. Demos is running a project on 'recapitalising the poor'. The New Economics Foundation has been working on new economic models, co-production and social return on investment. NCVO runs a Third Sector Foresight Programme which can be found on www.3s4.org.uk. Respublica is the home of the red Tories and provides a useful guide to progressive Conservative thinking.

references

Alinsky, S. (1972) *Rules for radicals: A political primer for practical radicals*, New York: Random House.

Allen, A. and May, C. (2007) *Setting up for success: A practical guide for community organisations*, London: Community Development Foundation.

Appiah, K.A. (2007) *The ethics of identity*, Princeton: Princeton University Press.

Arnstein, S. (1969) 'A ladder of participation in the USA', *Journal of the American Institute of Planners*, vol 35, July, pp 216–40.

Bachrach, P. and Baratz, M.S. (1962) 'Two faces of power', *American Political Science Review*, vol 56, pp 947–52.

Bandura, A. (1994) 'Self-efficacy', in H. Friedman (ed.) *Encyclopedia of mental health*, San Diego: Academic Press.

Banks, S. (2003) 'Introduction', in S. Banks, H. Butcher, P. Henderson and J. Robertson (eds) *Managing community practice*, Bristol: The Policy Press.

Banks, S., Butcher, H., Henderson, P. and Robertson, J. (eds) (2003) *Managing community practice: Principles, policies and programmes*, Bristol: The Policy Press.

Barr, A. and Hashagen, S. (2000) *ABCD handbook: A framework for evaluating community development*, London: Community Development Foundation.

Batten, T.R. and Batten, M. (1967) *The non-directive approach in group and community work*, London: Oxford University Press.

Blond, P. (2010) *Red Tory: How left and right have broken Britain and how we can fix it*, London: Faber and Faber.

Boal, A. (2008) *Theatre of the oppressed: Get political*, London: Pluto.

Bourdieu, P. (1986) 'The forms of capital', in J.G. Richardson (ed.), *Handbook of theory and research for the sociology of education*, New York: Greenwood Press, pp 241–58.

Bowles, M. (2008) *Democracy: the contribution of community development to local governance and democracy*, London: CDF.

Browne, J. and Levell, P. (2010) *The distributional effect of tax and benefit reforms to be introduced between June 2010 and April 2014: A revised assessment*, London: Institute of Fiscal Studies.

Burns, D. (2007) *Systemic action research*, Bristol: The Policy Press.

Burns, D. and Taylor, M. (1998) *Mutual aid and self-help: Coping strategies for excluded communities*, Bristol: The Policy Press.

Burns, D., Heywood, F., Taylor, M., Wilde, P. and Wilson, M. (2004) *Making community participation meaningful*, Bristol: The Policy Press.

Burrows, R., Ellison, N. and Woods, B. (2005) *Internet-based neighbourhood information systems and their consequences*, York: Joseph Rowntree Foundation.

Butcher, H., Banks, S., Henderson, P. and Robertson, J. (2007) *Critical community practice*, Bristol: The Policy Press.

Butcher, H., Glen, A., Henderson, P. and Smith, J. (eds) (1993) *Community and public policy*, London: Pluto Press.

Cabinet Office (2010) 'Building the Big Society', www.cabinetoffice.gov.uk/media/407789/building-big-society.pdf

Caniglia, B. and Carmin, J. (2005) 'Scholarship on social movement organizations: classic views and emerging trends', *Mobilization*, vol 10, no 2, pp 201–12.

Capra, F. (1996) *The web of life: A new synthesis of mind and matter*, London: HarperCollins.

Chambers, R. (1994) *World development*, Amsterdam: Elsevier.

Chanan, G. and Miller, C. (2009) *Empowerment skills for all*, Leeds: Homes and Communities Agency.

Clegg, S. (1989) *Frameworks of power*, London: Sage Publications.

CLES (Centre for Local Economic Strategies) (2009) *The importance of community anchor organisations to empowerment issues in the North West*, Stockport: NW Together We Can.

CLG (Communities and Local Government) (2006) *Community development challenge*, London: Communities and Local Government.

Coleman, J. (1990) *Foundations of social theory*, Cambridge, MA: Harvard University Press.

Commission on Integration and Cohesion (2007) *Our shared future: Final report of the Commission on Integration and Cohesion*, London: Communities and Local Government.

Community Development Exchange (2008) *What is community development?* Sheffield: CDX.

Cornwall, A. (2004) 'New democratic spaces? The politics and dynamics of institutionalised participation', *IDS Bulletin*, vol 35, no 2, pp 1–10.

Cox, E. and Schmueker, K. (2010) *Growing the Big Society: Encouraging success in social and community enterprise in deprived communities*, Newcastle: IPPR (north).

Craig, G. (2011) 'Introduction', in G. Craig, M. Mayo, K. Popple, M. Shaw and M. Taylor (eds) *Community development in the United Kingdom 1950–2010*, Bristol: Policy Press.

Craig, G. and Mak, H.W. (2007) *The Hong Kong Declaration: Building democratic institutions and civil society through community development, in the Asia-Pacific Region*, Hong Kong: IACD.

Craig, G., Gorman, M. and Vercseg, I. (2004) 'The Budapest declaration: building civil society through community development', *Community Development Journal*, vol 39, pp 423–9.

Craig, G., Mayo, M. and Taylor, M. (1990) 'Empowerment: a continuing role for community development', *Community Development Journal*, vol 25, no 4, pp 286–90.

Craig, G., Popple, K. and Shaw, M. (2008) *Community development in theory and practice*, Nottingham: Spokesman.

Craig, G., Mayo, M., Popple, K., Shaw, M. and Taylor, M. (eds) (2011) *Community development in the United Kingdom 1950–2010*. Bristol: Policy Press.

Crossley, N. (2002) *Making sense of social movements*, Buckingham: Open University Press.

De Filippis, J. (2007) 'Community development: the long view', in J. De Filippis and S. Saegert (eds) *The community development reader*, New York: Routledge, pp 29–35.

De Filippis, J. and Saegert, S. (2007) 'Conclusion', in J. De Filippis and S. Saegert (eds) *The community development reader*, New York: Routledge, pp 327–32.

DiMaggio, P. and Powell, W.W. (1983) 'The iron cage revisited: institutional isomorphism and collective rationality in organizational fields', *American Sociological Review*, vol 48, pp 459–62.

Dorsner, C. (2008) 'Implementing the Yaounde Declaration: practical issues on participatory processes in community development projects', *Community Development Journal*, vol 43, no 4, pp 413–27.

Driver, S. and Martell, L. (1997) 'New Labour's communitarianisms', *Critical Social Policy*, vol 17, no 3, pp 27–46.

Etzioni, A. (1998) *The essential communitarian reader*, Lanham, MD: Rowman & Littlefield.

FCDL (Federation for Commmunity Development Learning)(2009a) *National occupational standards for community development*, www.fcdl.org.uk/NOS_Consultation/Documents/NOS_CD_Eng_v2finalartworkedversion.pdf

FCDL (2009b) *Community work skills manual*, Sheffield: Federation of Community Work Learning.

Field, J. (2003) *Social capital*, London: Routledge.

Freire, P. (1972) *Pedagogy of the oppressed*, Harmondsworth: Penguin.

Gaventa, J. (2003) *Power after Lukes: A review of the literature*, Brighton: Institute of Development Studies.

Gilchrist, A. (2007) *Equalities and communities: Challenge, choice and change*, London: CDF.

Gilchrist, A. (2009) *The well-connected community: A networking approach to community development*, Bristol: Policy Press

Gilchrist, A., Wetherell, M. and Bowles, M. (2010) *Social action and identities: Connecting communities for a change*, Basingstoke: Open University Press.

Goetschius, G.W. (1969) *Working with community groups: Using community development as a method of social work*, London: Routledge.

Gramsci, A. (1992). *Prison notebooks* (Vol. 1), New York: Columbia University Press.

Granovetter, M. (1973) 'The strength of weak ties', *American Journal of Sociology*, vol 78, no 6, pp 1360–80.

Habermas, J. (1984) *The theory of communicative action. Vol. 1: Reason and rationalisation of society*, Cambridge: Polity.

Halpern, D. (2005) *Social capital*, Cambridge: Polity.

Hawtin, M. and Percy-Smith, J. (2007) *Community profiling: A practical guide*, Buckingham: Open University Press.

Henderson, P. and Vercseg, I. (2010) *Community development and civil society: Making connections in the European context*, Bristol: The Policy Press.

Hillery, G. (1955) 'Definitions of community: areas of agreement', *Rural Sociology*, vol 20, pp 111-23.

Hoggett, P., Mayo, M. and Miller, C. (2009) *The dilemmas of development work: ethnical challenges in regeneration*, Bristol: The Policy Press.

Howard, J. and Taylor, M. (2010) 'Hybridity in partnerships: managing tensions and opportunities', in D. Billis (ed.) *The erosion of the third sector? Hybrid organisations in a new welfare landscape*, London: Palgrave Macmillan.

Kretzmann, J. and McKnight, J. (1993) *Building communities from the inside out: A path toward finding and mobilizing a community's assets*, Evanston, IL: Institute for Policy Research, Northwestern University.

Kretzmann, J. and McKnight, J. (2003) Introduction to asset mapping, www..abcdinstitute.org/docs/abcd/IntroAssetMapping.pdf

Laclau, E. and Mouffe, C. (1985) *Hegemony and socialist strategy: Towards a radical democratic politics*, London: Verso.

Ledwith, M. (1997) *Participating in transformation: Towards a working model of community empowerment*, Birmingham: Venture Press.

Ledwith, M. (2005) *Community development: A critical approach*, Bristol: The Policy Press.

Ledwith, M. and Springett, J. (2010) *Participatory practice: Community based action for transformative change*, Bristol: The Policy Press.

Lipsky, M. (1980) *Street-level bureaucracy: Dilemmas of the individual in public services*, New York: Russell Sage Foundation.

Loney, M. (1983) *Community against government*, London: Heinemann.

Longstaff, B. (2008). *The community development challenge: Evaluation: Establishing an outcomes and evidence base*. London: Community Development Foundation.

Lukes, S. (2005) *Power: A radical view* (2nd edition), Basingstoke: Palgrave Macmillan.

Marris, P. and Rein, M. (1967) *Dilemmas of social reform*, New York: Atherton Press.

Marsh, D. and Rhodes, R. (1992) *Policy networks in British government*, Oxford: Oxford University Press.

Maslow, A. (1943) 'A theory of human motivation', *Psychological Review*, vol 50, no 4, pp 370–96.

Mayo, M. (1975) 'Community development: a radical alternative', in R. Bailey and M. Brake (eds) *Radical social work*, London: Arnold.

Mayo, M. (2005) *Global citizens: Social movements and the challenge of globalization*, London: Zed Press.

Mayo, M. (2008a) 'Introduction: community development: contestations, continuity and change' in G. Craig, K. Popple and M. Shaw (2008) *Community development in theory and practice: An international reader*, Nottingham: Spokesman.

Mayo, M. (ed) (2008b) *Active learning for active citizenship: And beyond?*, Leicester: NIACE Publications.

McAdam, D., McCarthy, J. and Zald, M. (1996) *Comparative perspectives on social movements*, Cambridge: Cambridge University Press.

Melucci, A. (1988) 'Social movements and the democratisation of everyday life', in J. Keane (ed.) *Civil society and the state*, London: Verso, pp 245–60.

Melucci, A. (1996) *Challenging codes: Collective action in the information age*, Cambridge: Cambridge University Press.

Miller, C. (2008) *The community development challenge: Management*, London: CDF.

Miller, P. and Rose, N. (2009) *Governing the present*, Cambridge: Polity Press.

Mouffe, C. (2005) *On the political: Thinking in action*, London: Routledge.

Nisbet, R. (1953) *The quest for community*, Oxford: Oxford University Press.

Noya, A., Clarence, E. and Craig, G. (eds) (2009) *Community capacity building: Creating a better future together*, Paris: OECD Publishing.

O'Connor, A. (2007) 'Swimming against the tide: a brief history of federal policy to poorer communities', in J. De Filippis and S. Saegert (eds) *The community development reader*, New York: Routledge, pp 9–27.

Pearce, J., Howard, J. and Bronstein, A. (2010) 'Editorial: learning from Latin America', *Community Development Journal*, vol 45, no 3, pp 265–76.

Pitchford, M. (2008) *Making spaces for community development*, Bristol, The Policy Press.

Plant, R. (1974) *Community and ideology: An essay in applied social philosophy*, London: Routledge & Kegan Paul.

Popple, K. (1995) *Analysing community work: Its theory and practice*, Buckingham: Open University Press.

Portes, A. (1995) 'Economic sociology and the sociology of immigration: a conceptual overview', in A. Portes (ed.), *The economic sociology of immigration*, New York: Russell Sage Foundation.

Pratchett, L., Durose, C., Lowndes, V., Stoker, G. and Wales, C. (2009) *Empowering communities to influence local decision making: A systematic review of the evidence*, London: Communities and Local Government.

Putnam, R. (1993) *Making democracy work*, Princeton, NJ: Princeton University Press.

Rabinow, P. (1984) 'Introduction', in P. Rabinow, (ed.) *The Foucault reader*, London: Penguin.

Rose, N. (1996) 'The death of the social', *Economy and Society*, vol 25, no 3, pp 327–56.

Rose, N. (1999) *Powers of freedom: Reframing political thought*, Cambridge: Cambridge University Press.

Rose, N. and Miller, P. (1992) 'Political power beyond the state: problematics of government', *British Journal of Sociology*, vol 43, pp 173–205.

Rothman, J. and Tropman, J. (1968) 'Three models of community organization practice', in *Social Work Practice 1968*, New York: Columbia University Press.

Rowan, L.., Papineschi, J., Taylor, S. and Gowing, E. (2009) *Third sector: Investment for growth*, Report for WRAP and REalliance.

Sabatier, P. (1988) 'An advocacy coalition framework of policy change and the role of policy-oriented learning therein', *Policy Sciences*, vol 21, pp 129–68.

Sampson, R. (2004) 'Neighbourhood and community: collective efficacy and community safety', *New Economy*, vol 11, pp 106–13.

Sampson, R. (2007, 'What community supplies', in J. De Filippis and S. Saegert (eds) *The Community development reader*, New York: Routledge, pp 163–173.

Sampson, R., Morenoff, J. and Gannon-Rowley, T. (2002) 'Assessing neighbourhood effects: social processes and new directions in research', *Annual Review of Sociology*, vol 28, pp 443–78.

Scott, M. (2010) *Unseen, unequal, untapped, unleashed: The potential for community action at the grassroots*, London: Community Sector Coalition.

Sen, A. (2009) *The idea of justice*, London: Allen Lane.

Sender, H., Carlisle, B., Hatamian, A. and Bowles, M. (2010) *Report on survey of community development practitioners and managers*, London: Community Development Foundation.

Seyfang, G. (2009) *The new economics of sustainable consumption*, Basingstoke: Palgrave.

Shaw, M. (2004) *Community work: Policy, politics and practice*, Hull: Universities of Hull and Edinburgh.

Shaw, M., Meagher, J. and Moir, S. (2006) *Participation in community development: Problems and possibilities*, Edinburgh: Concept with the Community Development Journal.

Skinner, S. and Farrar, G. (2009) *Liberating leadership: A fresh perspective*, London: Community Sector Coalition.

Skinner, S. and Wilson, M. (2002) *Assessing community strengths*, London: Community Development Foundation.

Smock, K. (2003) *Democracy in action: Community organizing and urban change*, New York: Columbia University Press.

Somerville, P. (2011) *Understanding community: Policy, politics and practice*, Bristol: The Policy Press.

Stoker, G. (1998) 'Governance as theory: five propositions', *International Social Science Journal*, vol 155, pp 17–28.

Somerville, P. (2011) *Understanding community: Politics, policy and practice*, Bristol: The Policy Press.

Tarrow, S. (1994) *Power in movement: Social movements, collective action and politics*, Cambridge: Cambridge University Press.

Taylor, M. (2003) *Public policy in the community*, Basingstoke: Palgrave Macmillan.

Taylor, M. (2007a) 'Community participation in the real world: opportunities and pitfalls in new governance spaces', *Urban Studies*, vol 44, no 2.

Taylor, M. (2007b) 'The nature of community organizing: social capital and community leadership', in R. Cnaan and C. Milofsky (eds) *The handbook of community movements and local organizations*, New York: Springer.

Taylor, M. (2010) *Community and public policy* (2nd edition), Bristol: The Policy Press.

Taylor, M., Barr, A. and West, A. (2000) *Signposts to community development* (2nd edition), London: Community Development Foundation.

Taylor, M., Wilson, M., Purdue, D. and Wilde, P. (2007) *Changing neighbourhoods: Lessons from the JRF Neighbourhoods Programme*, York: Joseph Rowntree Foundation.

Thake, S. (2001) *Building communities, changing lives: The contribution of large independent neighbourhood regeneration organisations*, York: Joseph Rowntree Foundation.

Twelvetrees, A. (2008) *Community work* (4th edition), Basingstoke: Palgrave Macmillan.

United Nations (1955) *Social progress through community development*, New York: United Nations.

Walker, G.P., Hunter, S., Devine-Wright, P., Evans, B. and Fay, H. (2007) 'Harnessing community energies: explaining and evaluating community-based localism in renewable energy policy in the UK', *Global Environmental Politics*, vol 7, no 2, 64–82.

Wellman, B. (1979) 'The community question: the intimate networks of East Yorkers', *American Journal of Sociology*, vol 84, no 5, pp 1201–31.

Wetherell, M. (2009a) *Theorizing identities and social action*, Basingstoke: Palgrave.

Wetherell, M. (2009b) *Identity in the 21st century: New trends in changing times*, Basingstoke: Palgrave.

Wind-Cowie, M. (2010) *Civic streets: The Big Society in action*, London: Demos.

Woodin, T., Crook, D. and Carpentier, V. (2010) *Community and mutual ownership: A historical review*, York: Joseph Rowntree Foundation.

Woolcock, M. (1998) 'Social capital and economic development: toward a theoretical synthesis and policy framework', *Theory and Society*, vol 27, no 2, pp 151–208.

World Commission on Environment and Development (1987) *Our common future* (The Brundtland Report), Oxford: Oxford University Press.

YHEP (Yorkshire & Humber Empowerment Partnership) (2010) 'Voices from Experience: empowering communities to improve their health and well-being', May, www.yhep.org.uk/resources/empowering-communities-improve-their-health-and-well-being

Young, M. and Willmott, P. (1962) *Family and kinship in East London* (2nd edition), London: Institute of Community Studies.

appendix

The main community development organisations in the UK

Action with Communities in Rural England (ACRE)
Somerford Court, Somerford Road, Cirencester, GL7 ITW
Telephone: 01285 653477
www.acre.org.uk/

ACRE is active in promoting the interests of rural communities. It also acts as the national umbrella organisation for 38 Rural Community Councils throughout England. ACRE aims to promote a healthy, vibrant and sustainable rural community sector that is well connected to policies and initiatives at national, regional, subregional and local levels. ACRE's organisational vision is to provide a rural community development centre of expertise that is extensively used by policy makers and practitioners.

Community Development Cymru (CDC)
Plas Dolerw, Milford Road, Newtown, Powys SY16 2EH
Telephone: 01686 627377
www.cdcymru.org/

CDC is an all-Wales member-led independent organisation. It aims to work across sectors to: develop a common understanding of the values and practice principles of community development; promote community development at all levels, throughout Wales; strengthen support for community development workers and others engaged in community development; play an active role in the advancement of standards in community development practice; and facilitate the development of a collective voice in communicating about community development at all levels (including policy) for Wales.

Community Development Exchange (CDX)
Scotia Works, Leadmill Road, Sheffield SI 4SE
Telephone: 0114 270 1718
www.cdx.org.uk

CDX is the UK-wide membership organisation for community development. It works to ensure that community development is recognised and supported as a powerful way of tackling inequality and achieving social justice. As an organisation with members from across the UK, CDX reflects a diverse range of interests in community development across all sectors and fields.

Community Development Foundation (CDF)
Unit 5, Angel Gate, 320–326 City Road, London EC1V 2PT
Telephone: 020 7833 1772
www.cdf.org.uk

CDF is a leading source of intelligence, guidance and delivery on community development in England and across the UK.

Community Development Society International (CDSI)
www.comm-dev.org

CDSI is US-based but with members throughout the world. It organises international conferences and publishes a journal.

Community Links
105 Barking Road, Canning Town, London E16 4HQ
Telephone: 020 7473 2270
www.community-links.org

Community Links is an innovative inner city charity running community-based projects in east London. Founded in 1977; it now helps over 50,000 vulnerable children, young people and adults every year, with most of its work delivered in Newham, one of the poorest boroughs in Europe. Its successes influence both community-based organisations nationwide and government policy.

Community Matters
12–20 Baron Street, London N1 9LL
Telephone: 020 7837 7887
www.communitymatters.org.uk

Community Matters is the national federation for community organisations. It currently has 1,156 member organisations across the UK and has been supporting community associations and similar organisations since 1945.

Community Workers' Co-operative (CWC)
CWC National Office, Unit 4 First Floor, Tuam Road Centre,
Tuam Road, Galway
Telephone: +353 (0) 91 779 030

CWC is a national organisation that promotes and supports community work across for the whole of the island of Ireland. It was established in 1981 and currently has 800 members.

Federation for Community Development Learning
3rd Floor, The Circle Building, 33 Rockingham Lane, Sheffield S1 4FW
Telephone: 0114 253 6770
www.fcdl.org.uk

The UK-wide network for community development training, supporting the development of communities through advancing and promoting community work learning at local, regional and national levels and the creation of appropriate opportunities for training and qualification.

Federation of City Farms and Community Gardens (FCFCG)

The Green House, Hereford Street, Bristol BS3 4NA
Telephone: 0117 923 1800
www.farmgarden.org.uk

FCFCG is the representative body for city farms, community gardens and similar community-led organisations in the UK. It promotes and represents its members at a national, regional and local level. It also provides a wide range of services, advice and support for city farms and community gardens, whether they are well established or just getting off the ground.

International Association for Community Development (IACD)

The Stables, Falkland, Fife KY15 7AF
www.iacdglobal.org

IACD is an international not-for-profit, non-government membership organisation committed to building a global network of people and organisations working toward social justice through community development. It has members in 70 countries worldwide.

Locality

33 Corsham Street, London, N1 6DR
Telephone: 0845 241 0375

Locality is the new national network of settlements, development trusts, social action centres and community enterprises, formed from the merger of bassac (the British Association of Settlements and Social Action Centres) and the Development Trusts Association. It works with members on community asset ownership, collaboration, commissioning support, social enterprise, community voice and advocacy.

The National Association for Voluntary and Community Action (NAVCA)

The Tower, 2 Furnival Square, Sheffield S1 4QL
Telephone: 0114 278 6636
www.navca.org.uk

NAVCA (is the national voice of local voluntary and community sector infrastructure in England. Its 360 members work with 140,000 local community groups and voluntary organisations which provide services, regenerate neighbourhoods, increase volunteering and tackle discrimination, in partnership with local public bodies.

Novas Scarman

73–81 Southwark Bridge Road
London SE1 0NQ
Telephone: 020 7939 9720
www.novasscarman.org

Novas Scarman is a national charity committed to helping citizens bring about change in their community, in the way that they give practical assistance to hundreds of remarkable people with a 'can do' attitude. These 'can do-ers' in their turn mobilise many thousands of others, within their own communities and across the major institutions of society – working to make fundamental life chances available to all.

Scottish Community Development Centre (SCDC)

Suite 305, Baltic Chambers, 50 Wellington Street, Glasgow G2 6HJ
Telephone: 0141 248 1924
www.scdc.org.uk

SCDC is the designated national development centre for community development in Scotland. It is an innovative partnership between the Community Development Foundation (a UK non-departmental public body funded by government to support community development) and the University of Glasgow. Its main function is the delivery of a range of large-scale contracts on behalf of national agencies such as

Communities Scotland, NHS Health Scotland, Greenspace Scotland, Scottish Natural Heritage and the Carnegie Trust.

Scottish Community Development Network (SCDN)

PO Box 26792, Glasgow G4 7AF
No telephone
www.scdn.org.uk

SCDN is a member-led organisation for community workers and community development workers, paid or unpaid, full or part time, from the community, voluntary or public sectors, who support the principles and practice of community development.

Take Part Network

www.takepart.org

The Take Part Network has grown out of the CLG Take Part programme, which ends in March 2011 (which itself grew out of the Active Learning for Active Citizenship initiative). It promotes a distinctive approach to learning that enables people to make an active contribution to their communities and influence public policies and services. This focuses on community-based learning, open dialogue and reflection, aimed at giving people an understanding of how power works and how they can learn to influence decisions and policies.

Ubuntu

c/o FCDL, 3rd Floor, The Circle Building, 33 Rockingham Lane, Sheffield S1 4FW
Telephone: 0114 253 6770
www.fcdl.org.uk/Ubuntu/index.htm

The interest group for black and minority ethnic community workers and activists supported by the Federation for Community Development Learning.

Urban Forum
33 Corsham Street, London N1 6DR
Telephone: 020 7253 4816
www.urbanforum.org.uk

Urban Forum is a national charity and a membership organisation that supports communities to have a greater say over the decisions that affect them. By gathering evidence and feedback from its members, the organisation acts as a bridge between policy makers and community groups operating on the ground.

Opportunities for further study and training

There are a number of courses in the UK which support learning on community development, some of which lead to a professional qualification. The courses in youth and community (which are mostly at degree level) can be found through the websites of the National Youth Agency (www.nya.org.uk). In England, the Endorsement and Quality Standrds Board for Community Development Learning (www. esbendorsement.org) provides information about training based on the national occupational standards for community development work. These include work-based and Foundation degrees.

LifelongLearning UK (www.lluk.org) is the national skills council that covers community development and lists a range of courses (see Table A1). Some of these are offered on both full-time and part-time bases.

In addition, there are a number of short courses, including one-day workshops, which provide taster sessions or very specific skills-based learning. You can find out about these from the websites of organisations such as the Federation for Community Development Learning, the National Association for Voluntary and Community Action, Tenants Participation Advisory Service, the Community Development Exchange, and others listed in this appendix.

Table A1: Community development courses in the UK (as of April 2010)

Delivery centre	Validating higher education institution	Course title and qualifications offered
The University of Bradford	The University of Bradford	Community Regeneration and Development
Bradford College	Bradford College: An Associate College of Leeds Metropolitan	Youth and Community Development BA(Hons); Community Development Work FdA
The University of Huddersfield	The University of Huddersfield	Community Studies BA (Hons)
Sheffield Hallam University	Sheffield Hallam University	Youth and Community Work BA (Hons)
University of Sunderland	University of Sunderland	Community and Youth Work Studies BA (Hons)
Aberdeen College Gallowgate Centre	CeVe	Working with Communities HNC
University of Aberdeen	University of Aberdeen	Certificate in Adult and Community Learning
University of Dundee	University of Dundee	Community Education BA (Hons)
University of Ulster	University of Ulster	Community Development BSc (Hons)
Bangor University (was University of Wales, Bangor)	Bangor University	Community Development FdA, HE Cert
University of Glamorgan, Cardiff and Pontypridd	University of Glamorgan, Cardiff and Pontypridd	Public Services BA (Hons)
Department of Voluntary Sector Studies	University of Wales Lampeter	Voluntary Sector Studies BA (Hons)

Delivery centre	Validating higher education institution	Course title and qualifications offered
University of Wales, Newport	University of Wales, Newport	Youth and Community Studies BA (Hons)
Glyndwr University	Glyndwr University	Community Studies FdA; Youth and Community Studies BA (Hons)
Trinity College Carmarthen	Trinity College Carmarthen	BA /FdA Community Development
University of East London	University of East London	BA (Hons) Community Studies;
Goldsmiths College (University of London)	Goldsmiths College (University of London)	Access to Dip HE in community and youth Work;
		BA (Hons) Applied Social Science;
		M.Phil/PhD Community and Youth Work;
		Community Development and Youth Work;
		Dip HE Community Work
University of Greenwich	University of Greenwich	Youth and Community Studies BA (Hons); Dip HE
Havering College of Further and Higher Education	Havering College (Open University)	Youth and Community Work BA (Hons); Dip HE
YMCA George Williams College	Canterbury Christchurch University	BA Hons/Dip HE in informal education (youth work and community learning and development
University of Bedfordshire	University of Bedfordshire	Youth and Community Studies BA (Hons)
Bournemouth University	Bournemouth University	Community Work BA (Hons)

Delivery centre	Validating higher education institution	Course title and qualifications offered
University of Chichester	University of Chichester	Youth and Community Work BA (Hons)
Mid-Kent College, Chatham	The University of Kent	Community Development and Regeneration FdA
Ruskin College Oxford	Ruskin College (Open University)	Youth and Community Work BA (Hons)
De Montfort University	De Montfort University	Youth and Community Development BA (Hons); DipHE
University of Derby	University of Derby	Voluntary and Community Sector Management Hons FdA; Community Development and Regeneration FdA; Voluntary Sector and Volunteering - University Certificate; Applied Community Work BA
University of Northampton	University of Northampton	Social and Community Development BA (Hons)
Coventry University	Coventry University	Social Welfare and Community Studies BA (Hons)
Staffordshire University	Staffordshire University	Community Learning FdA
South Devon College	University of Plymouth	Young People and Community Service FdA
Truro College	University of Plymouth	Community Studies (Development and Youth Work) FdSc
The University of Bolton	The University of Bolton	Community Studies / Applied Community Studies BA (Hons)

Delivery centre	Validating higher education institution	Course title and qualifications offered
University of Central Lancashire	University of Central Lancashire	Volunteering & Community Action Foundation Degree; Active Citizenship and Volunteer Development BA (Hons)
Liverpool John Moores University	Liverpool John Moores University	Applied Community and Social Studies BA (Hons)
The University of Manchester	The University of Manchester	Applied Community and Youth Work Studies BA (Hons)
Lancaster	University of Cumbria	Youth and Community Development BA (Hons); Dip HE

index

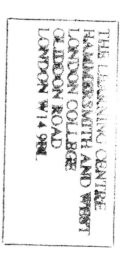